Life
Ever Laughter

God Bless you

Jerry Clower

D1166116

JERRY CLOWER

Life Ever Laughter

THE HEART AND HUMOR
OF JERRY CLOWER

RUTLEDGE HILL PRESS
Nashville, Tennessee

Copyright © 1987 by Jerry Clower

All rights reserved. Written permission must be secured from the publisher to use or reproduce any part of this book, except for brief quotations in critical reviews or articles.

Published in Nashville, Tennessee, by Rutledge Hill Press, Inc., 513 Third Avenue South, Nashville, Tennessee 37210.

Typography: ProtoType Graphics, Inc., Nashville, Tennessee
Design: Harriette Bateman
Printed by R.R. Donnelley & Sons
Special thanks to Brent D. Holmes for developing the title of this book: *Life EverLaughter*

Library of Congress Cataloging-in-Publication Data

Clower, Jerry, 1926–
    Life everlaughter: the heart and humor of Jerry Clower.
        p.   cm.
    ISBN 1-55853-070-3
    1. Clower, Jerry, 1926–   . 2. Comedians—United States—
Biography. I. Title. II. Title: Life ever laughter.
PN2287.C547A3   1987
818'.5402—dc19   87-22318
                                                                                         CIP

Manufactured in the United States of America
4 5 6 7 8 9 — 93 92 91 90

Contents

Foreword

It's been nine years since the last book . . . eight albums, sixteen hundred concerts, two additional grandchildren and more mileage than Jerry wants to remember. Another spell of explaining that passage of time just had to be.

Care to join me in *Life EverLaughter* to share some musings and happenings? I'd be some kind of glad to have you. I'm going to start off with a little bit about me, my family, my work, and some pictures from the family album. Then the book rambles over things a person contemplates when he has his hands working and his mind wandering. . . . And, of course, I've included some stories old and new. Tandy Rice, my friend and manager, tossed in some letters and nice things folks have said about me; Homerline and Big Mama contributed some recipes.

You know I've always said there's only one place where there is no laughter, and that's hell. I have made arrangements to miss hell. Praise God, I won't ever have to be anywhere that there ain't no laughter.

Jerry Clower

Life
Ever Laughter

From Route 4 and Back Again

Y ou know, thirty years ago if you'd told me this boy from
Route 4, Liberty, Mississippi, would be sitting in his
agent's office contemplating putting the facts of his life together into a book—for the third time—I'd have been flabber-
gasted.

But I start each day saying, "Lord, I am on your side. You
ain't never made a mistake, so whatever happens in my life today,
I'll just praise your Holy Name and keep goin'." That's a simple
thing to do, but it works.

Now I know I already wrote down some of this stuff in *Ain't
God Good* and *Let the Hammer Down*, but that was nine or ten years
ago and I've met a lot of people since then who want to know how I
got to being what I am—a country comedian with a real zest for
living. So if you happen to have read those other books, you can
skip to the next chapter—unless you want to take a look at some of
my family-album kind of pictures.

I'll tell the truth about my growing up. I did admire my 4-H
agent, Monroe McElveen, and I thought I wanted to be doing the
kind of work he was doing—working with boys and girls who really
appreciated a helping hand. Back in Amite (pronounced ā-mīt´)
County, Mississippi, "Red" McElveen disciplined me. He did
some of the things a father would have done. I remember one time a
bunch of us 4-H kids went out to Percy Quin State Park not too far
from Liberty. I was a daredevil back then, and I just went running
to the lake and dived right in. Mr. McElveen blew his whistle and
said firmly, "Jerry, this is the buddy system. You and Larry swim
together, and if I blow a whistle and you cannot touch the top of
Larry's head in one second, you're getting out and going back to
the tent."

"I can swim. Don't need anybody to look after me."

"Yeah, well, we know you're a good swimmer. You could
probably win the Olympics, but if you swim here today, you're
going to do it by the buddy system."

After the second day, I discovered keeping up with a buddy
was fun.

Mr. McElveen taught me other things, too. Through his leadership I learned how to judge seed, field crops, and milk cows. When I went on to Mississippi State, I found out he had taught me a whole lot of basics. Yes, I wanted to be like Mr. McElveen when I grew up, and the fact that he was a football hero made him even more outstanding. During his days at Mississippi State, he had intercepted a pass against Auburn University and run it ninety-seven yards for a touchdown in the university's first-ever win over that strong team.

It wasn't 'til I got out of high school and then the Navy I figured out that what I had to do to follow in Red McElveen's footsteps was to get a degree in agriculture.

Now I'd been a *B* student in high school—could have reached for *A*'s but there was too much else going on at my stepfather's farm. You see, when I was real young, Mama made a decision to part from my father Otha (everybody called him Buster) Clower after he'd disappointed her more than enough. Buster was a truck driver, but during the Depression he went up to Memphis to look for work in the railroad shops, joined a fraternal order and got to drinking and forgetting family responsibilities.

For a while there were just the three of us—Mama, not but seventeen years older than I was, myself, and my brother, Sonny.

Monroe McElveen, my 4-H leader, inspired me to get a degree in agriculture and taught me discipline.

My mother, Mable Moore,
"Big Mama" to all her family.

We all three went back to live in my grandaddy's house on Route 4 in Liberty, Mississippi. Grandpa had a forty-acre farm. Mama worked so hard picking cotton sometimes the blood would ooze from her fingertips. Later on she took a job in town. She was a woman who knew what loving and caring for her family meant. That goodness might just have been inherited from her father, Wesley Burns. He was the kindest man anyone ever did meet—died without a thing because he gave away whatever he managed to get.

My mother, Mabel Burns Clower, met my stepfather, Elliott Moore, when he was visiting town as a student at Southwest Junior College. Some of the boys would come "gal-ing" as they called it. When he and Mama got married, Elliott Moore borrowed enough money from a bank in Magnolia, Mississippi, to get us a house and two hundred acres, so we moved out of my grandpa's up the road to our place.

My stepfather was a plasterer. He'd travel to jobs as needed—sometimes to Natchez, McComb, or Baton Rouge, and he clear-as-day needed help on the farm. Sonny fed the mules and I did the milking with the cow's tail full of cockleburs hitting me beside the head. If we didn't do a job right, Elliott Moore let us know about it. We rounded up hogs after a break-out, tended crops with a couple of hands, cut stove wood. We lived simple . . . drew bath water out of the reservoir and used a two-holed privy. We had a pond with

13

About 1938 (left) my brother, Sonny, had me by a head. Ten years later, I had reduced the size differential considerably.

plenty of catfish in it. My stepfather used a firm, loving hand with us and I'm grateful for his care.

Riding the school bus, working, being motivated to produce enough coins to get to the movies once in a while, and toeing the line drawn by my stepfather kept Sonny and me pretty busy. That is not to say we didn't have fun. We used to skin off our overalls (and we didn't have anything on underneath 'cause our mother said the overalls would fade on our underwear). Then we'd jump twenty feet down into a swimming hole hollering like Tarzan. That was pretty close to pure bliss for an Amite County boy. Coon hunts, candy pullings, rat killings and logrolling brought us all pleasure.

And I'll tell you what else was fun . . . a rainy afternoon with just enough rain to soak the ground so you couldn't plow. We'd sit on the porch and hear the rain slapping on that galvanized tin roof. Mama would bring us some dry clothes to put on—really just rags; she would cut us a watermelon, and we'd sit out on the back porch eating that melon. Then it would quit raining but stay cloudy, cool, and wet enough so we didn't have to go back to work. We'd call the dogs and go out rabbit hunting. If we got one, Mama would prepare it and make some biscuits and some old sawmill gravy. Between the watermelon, the rabbit stew, and no-plowing, a rainy day did make for good times.

14

East Fork School picture, 1938.

East Fork School was a white, wooden building with shiplap sides, a study hall in the middle of its *U* shape and four rooms for the elementary grades on one side, four rooms for the high school students on the other. Elementary grades were doubled up, two to a room with anywhere from eight to sixteen students for the two grades put together. When we got to high school, we used the study hall, too. Mrs. Ray J. Turner was my favorite high school teacher— English and diction. I never heard the words *current events* 'til I got to her class. We would go to somebody's house and borrow a newspaper, and I learned the importance of knowing what's going on beyond our own small world. There were just eight people in my high school graduating class. My brother and I had to listen to high school football games over the radio from McComb, Meridian, or Memphis to satisfy our need for *organized* contact sport.

Right after high school, I went into the Navy just like my brother, Sonny. He spent the war in submarines and I ended up in the Combat Intelligence Center on an aircraft carrier in the Pacific. I learned a lot in the service about machines and sea-going and people. Where I come from, you were either black or white; if you were white, you knew you were better than black. It took some boys from the North at a naval base in Virginia to teach me there were all kinds of people you could be better than. I mean to tell you I learned a lot—and with the help of a number of good people, I have unlearned bigotry. More about that later.

I remember the day I got home from the Navy. Right away Mama wanted to know. what I planned for my future. Well, by then, I knew two things. I wanted to play football and I wanted to get a degree in agriculture so I could work for the 4-H.

It turned out I did both. I played football at Southwest Mississippi Junior College in Summit even though I'd never played a game in my life. The first game I ever saw, I played in. I visited the coach just before school started. He looked at my six-foot, 214-pound body and believed me enough when I said I was ready to play to give me a half-scholarship. After two years there, I moved on to Mississippi State where I lettered playing in the Southeastern Conference. Whoooeee! I'm glad I had that opportunity.

Then I got my degree in agriculture and a job as assistant county agent in charge of 4-H Club work at Oxford, Mississippi, in 1951. Homerline and I had been married in 1947, so we moved up to Oxford and life was rolling along just fine. Young Ray entered the world on Valentine's Day in 1953 and Homerline introduced us to Amy in 1955. (Daughters Sue and Katy later joined us in 1962 and 1970 respectively.) By that time I had gone to work for Mr. Owen Cooper, president of the Mississippi Chemical Company. That wonderful man unlearned my bigotry and gave me a professional home for seventeen years. I became a director of field services for him; that's a high-falutin' way of saying fertilizer salesman.

When I was in the Navy, I attended radio school at Miami University, Oxford, Ohio.

My mama says she can't remember a time when I wasn't talking. In high school and in the Navy I spent a lot of time telling stories and having fun with them. I didn't make them up. They just seemed to be there in my head. When I discovered people bought more fertilizer if I threw in a couple of stories, the swap seemed more than fair. Folks at the Cattlemen's Association or the Farm Bureau listened to homogenized, palletized, homogenous fertilizer talk all right but they invited me back when I blended in some good humor. Those talks led to a dare by a Lubbock, Texas, disk jockey and a record that got played by directors of farm radio shows all over the country . . . and eventually MCA records heard me. I sure hadn't planned it—and it required the patience and cooperation of Mr. Owen Cooper and Mr. Charles Jackson at Mississippi Chemical before I would become a comedian full time. Instead of director of field services, I stayed on as sales promotion director by mutual agreement. I make occasional public appearances for that fine company even now.

The rest of the time I travel two hundred days of the year with about a month off around Christmas time. When I look back through the appointment book my secretary, Judy Moore of Yazoo City, has kept for years, it's a little like rolling a film. Here's a sample month of travel:

March 1:   Sutherland Lumber taping
             JAXN taping
March 2:   Farmers Union, Washington, D.C.
March 3-6:   SEC, Lexington, KY
March 4:   Prayer Breakfast
March 8:   Civic Arena, Baltimore, with Jeannie C. Riley
March 10:   Pascagoula, MS
March 11:   Kenansville, NC
March 12-13: Grand Ole Opry
March 15-18: Fort Walton Beach, FL
March 18:   Biloxi, MS
March 19:   East Fork, MS
March 24:   radio spots
March 25:   Angleton, TX
March 26-29: New Orleans, LA
March 31:   Tallahassee, FL

Randy Owen, Jeff Cook, Mark Herndon, and Teddy Gentry of Alabama received Country Music Association's award for Vocal Group of the Year from me . . . a grand night for all of us.

Flipping through those appointment books conjures up a lot of memories.

In 1977 or 1978, I was visiting all the radio stations in Myrtle Beach, South Carolina. Everywhere I stopped an old, beat-up van full of kids would follow—from one station to the next. At the last station I pulled over and approached the van.

"You boys come on in here now. You've been following me all over town so you must be serious about wanting to talk to me."

"We've been listening to your records all our lives, and when we heard you were in town, we just had to meet you," said the group's spokesman.

I found out those boys had a band that set up on the beaches and played right out on the sand for whatever people would flip them. It was a real pleasure to present that group, ALABAMA, a Country Music Association Award not too long after. You could say they have done right well.

Doing "Country Crossroads," a half-hour country music show has been a boon and a blessing to me. I have co-hosted the radio program with Bill Mack for about twenty years.

In 1983, with 1400 radio stations nationwide, the show expanded into the world of cable TV on ACTS, the Southern Baptist Radio and Television Commission network. The radio program today serves 2900 stations every week.

I remember one time I was driving in the back seat of a taxi from the Hot Springs airport to a speaking engagement in town. My driver began telling me that her family listens to "Country Crossroads" every Sunday afternoon, and they don't let the doorbell or the telephone's ringing interrupt.

"Why not?" I asked.

"My husband heard you talking so much over that program about what Christianity means to you, he decided there might be something to it. So he started going to church and then joined. I had sort of gotten away from it myself, but when I went back to church, then so did our two boys, our married daughter, my son-in-law, his parents, and his brother."

Hearing that good woman's story makes up for all the miles I have ever traveled back and forth to Fort Worth to do the show.

In 1984, New Orleans put on a World's Fair and created a whole day just for me. Someone suggested I was getting pretty emotional about it so I had to just tell them "I grew up about 100 miles up the railroad track from here in the Depression without a daddy. I used to pray that someday I might just get to *come* to New Orleans. So, yeah, I'm emotional over Jerry Clower Day at this World's Fair."

In the summer of 1985 I discovered an entire town of new kinfolk in Livingston County, Kentucky, when I visited Ledbetter: population, 280. Residents there held a Ledbetter Homecoming, a city-wide celebration with games, a Marcel Ledbetter look-alike contest, and dinner on the grounds. Officials even dismissed school for part of the day. I do like small towns—and especially ones full of Ledbetters!

In 1986, Yazoo City, Mississippi, named a broad section of highway after me, an event covered by most of the news media in

19

Homerline, my grandson Jayree, and I arrive at ceremonies celebrating the opening of Yazoo City's Jerry Clower Boulevard.

Mississippi and some of the national networks. Sure is good to have Homerline around to keep me from getting long-headed. That woman is full of wisdom.

I've been fortunate enough to have my work recognized by *Billboard Magazine, Music City News, Record World,* and *Cashbox* and I appreciate all those awards, but the grandest one may have been announced by *Music City News* during Fan Fair Week in 1987. It read, "*Music City News* salutes Jerry Clower for his outstanding service to humanity; for his promotion of country music; and for leaving laughter and love as his legacy." I'm proud of that.

Sometimes I think I'm the luckiest guy in the world. I've been married to the same woman for forty years I have four head of young'uns plus three grandchildren. I've been with the same record label since I entered show business. I have the same agency and the same manager. No one could have been more blessed.

About a year ago I got to thinking about Route 4, Liberty, Mississippi; it dawned on me that a fellow could go back and expe-

Mayor Charles E. (Blackie) Fulgham gave me my own highway marker. I called my first album "Jerry Clower From Yazoo City, Mississippi, Talkin'" and I have been proud to mention the city's name ever since.

rience some of the better old traditions. I knew for sure if I ever went back, I wanted a house with a porch on it so we could sit and listen to the rain on the roof—maybe even have some watermelon with our East Fork kin. Well, an architect is coming up with the design and the last chicken is about to fly from the nest, so that's what Homerline and I are planning. We're going back to Route 4, Liberty, Mississippi. Two hundred days on the road, one hundred sixty-five in Liberty.

Home again, home again, back to Amite.
Home again, home again, that's where we'll git.
The river's still flowin'. I trust the fish bite.
Home again, home again, sure will feel right.

My First Banana

A lot of things happened on Route 4, Mississippi. I remember the first banana I ever saw. I was nearly a grown boy fixing to go off to the United States Navy. Marcel and I caught the train at McComb, Mississippi, and went to Williamsburg, Virginia, to serve our country and go to boot camp. Some French-speaking folks had driven up to Liberty from Louisiana and brought a big bunch of bananas and swapped it for a coon dog. Well, Mama fixed us a beautiful lunch and put some bananas in there for us to go off to war. We had been on the train about eight hours when Marcel got hungry. Mama had told us to take that yellow part off that banana before we ate any of it. Marcel removed that yellow part, took a big bite and just as he bit that banana we went into a tunnel. And Marcel said, "Jerry, Jerry, ooo, Jerry, have you eaten your banana yet?" I said, "No." He said, "Well, don't. I took one bite of mine and went stone blind."

I don't care how good you can pick a guitar, how good you can sing, how good you can tell a story, how good you can perform . . . if you still ain't good people, you ain't nothing.

Dogs I Have Known

S everal dogs have contributed to my life, and all of them have made my life happier. Right now I have a four-legged canine the likes of which I said I'd never own. In the first place, she's a house dog and in the second place, she thinks she's people—a regular lap dog. We got her because I was put between a rock and a hard place.

A couple of years ago a lady in Okolona, Mississippi, wrote me: "Dear Jerry, please don't rob me of the thrill and the blessing I will receive by denying me the right to give your little girl a poodle dog."

Well, she done knocked me in the creek. If I had said, "No, Katy, you can't have this dog," then I would have been just an old, mean, bad fellow. And if I had said "no" to this lady, I would have deprived her of the blessing of giving.

Good gracious.

The letter continued: "I want to give Katy a puppy, a registered black toy French poodle of world-famous blood lines. Its mother had her picture on the front page of the Madison Square Garden dog show program. This dog's papa was Guy de Pierre de Mokosho de Booshwa Sheebedo."

"Mercy," I thought.

"And this dog's mama was some kind of de Booshwa de Bishoo."

I said, "Good gracious alive."

I just wrote the lady and said, "Yes." Sometimes it's better not to ask why. Sometimes it's better not to run things through your family. You just go ahead and suffer the consequences if it isn't the right thing to do.

We went to Okolona, Mississippi, with Katy to get this world-famous puppy, shared a catfish dinner with the donor, and started back home with the puppy.

"What are we going to name this dog?" Katy asked.

Well, the registration papers indicated the dog needed several names so as to avoid duplication with some other registered animal.

We named this little black poodle "Tandy Rice Katy Burns Marcel Ledbetter Freckles." We call her "Freckles." She's a regular member of my family.

If you get the car keys from their hook on the wall, Freckles will walk on her hind legs, just yapping for a ride. If you say, "You can't go," she'll fall to the floor and pout just like a young'un.

When I'm home Freckles sits in my lap a lot of the time. We watch television together and read the newspaper, but I'll give you $100 if you can throw that dog in my wife's lap.

That dog is not allowed on the couch, but when my wife walks down the hall to the bedroom, Freckles will jump up on the couch and run from one end to the other, then stand on her hind legs and watch down the hall. When she hears my wife coming, she'll jump off that couch and lie down on the floor like she's never been up there. That dog is smart! But I hope to the Lord my grandpa doesn't know I've got a lap dog—and that I let it in the house!

Mike, a big old white American pit bulldog helped raise me. My brother, Sonny, and I would catch that school bus and old Mike would stand there watching us ride off. When we got back that evening, old Mike would be right back out there lying in the yard, watching that gravel road and waiting for us to get off. When my mama wanted to chastise us, she had to shut old Mike up in the milk barn because he wouldn't let her put a hand on us.

Sonny and I could never get away with leaving a posthole digger, a maul, or a roll of barbed wire out in the field. We'd be eating supper and Mike wouldn't show up. Mama would say, "Y'all left somethin'. Go back out there and get whatever tools you left."

We'd go back to wherever we had been working, and old Mike would be lying down by that tool. He would not come to the house if we left something in the field. Old Mike had a great part in my upbringing.

You know I've been right lucky that coon hunting and dogs have been good to me. When I was a boy we had a pack of hounds. Old Queen, a one-eyed red bone, was the mama of most of 'em. Then there was old Torry, another red bone hound; Highball (more

Tandy Rice Katy Burns Marcel Ledbetter Freckles and me.

about Highball later); and Brummin, a huge, muscular, black and tan dog who barked like thunder. And he didn't bark at anything but coons.

I remember one day we had come in from the field we'd been plowing all morning. We were sitting around the table where Mama had put corn bread, peas, and a big old bowl of boiled okra—slick, slimy, boiled okra. When we finished dinner that day, Mama said, "Jerry, go feed the dogs."

Well, there was nothing left but that big old bowl of boiled okra so I picked it up, careful not to let that slimy, slick boiled okra run over on my hand and walked out in the back yard. Those dogs started running after me until I dumped that bowl of boiled okra in the dog pan. Old Brummin rammed his mouth down on it and said, "SSSHHHHHH'OOPP" . . . just sucked it all up. That okra was so slick, he just inhaled it all in one breath. It went down so fast, Brummin thought the other dog had gotten it and jumped on him. Those dogs fought the rest of the evening and didn't but one dog know what they were fighting about.

I was introduced to a beautiful pit bullterrier, Nicki, when I made a Purina Dog Chow commercial at Vanderbilt football stadium. The folks from Hollywood instructed me to lead this dog across the field and do a couple of things with him. That dog worked by the day just like I did . . . a real professional. But I didn't realize how important Nicki was until I started getting letters.

About a month before the Purina commercial ran, I had the privilege of doing a ninety-minute CBS special with the Oak Ridge Boys, Loretta Lynn, Charlie Pride, and Tom T. Hall. Man, millions of people watched that "Orange Blossom Special," and when it was all over, I got seven letters complimenting me.

A month later this thirty-second Purina Dog Chow commercial ran. *Thirty seconds* versus *ninety minutes* on national television. I got 107 letters wanting to know what that dog's name was, what kind of disposition he had, what he was really like, etcetera, etcetera. Well, I had to answer those letters and in finding out about the dog, we learned that Nicki was the dog that had ridden in the jeep next to George C. Scott playing General Patton. Nicki was more world-famous than I was. That doggoned experience was kinda humbling. Four legs draw better than two any day.

Highball was the greatest coon dog that ever lived. One evening we were coon hunting down in the swamps and old Queen struck a cold trail. Brummin bellered like thunder and it wasn't very long before they barked as if they could actually see a coon. We got up there and a great big hollow tree had been blown over and in that hollow tree sat a powerful old coon—Old Slant Face.

Uncle Versie Ledbetter had been trying to catch this big old coon forever. And when we caught up, Uncle Versie said, "Sic him," and a couple of the young dogs ran up in the tree, and that old coon just sat back on his hind legs and slapped those young dogs; they came out of there howling. Directly, Uncle Versie said, "Boys, we got to turn old Highball loose and let him bring that coon out of there."

Highball pounced up in that hollow tree, and you never heard such a ruckus and a racket in your life. He and the coon came rolling out of that hollow log, wallowing down sweet gum bushes, and all the time Uncle Versie was yelling, "You can do it, Highball, you can do it. Put it to him Highball, put it to him." Ooooohhhhh, you could hear him holler all over those swamps.

Now running down the middle of that swamp was a railroad, and old Highball and that old coon struggled until they ended up on that railroad just in time for the Midnight Express, a long banana train. With the wind blowing in the wrong direction, we couldn't hear that train. Before we knew it, here came that train—wham!—and ran over the coon and Highball. Killed both of 'em graveyard dead.

Uncle Versie started squalling, mopping the tears with his bandana handkerchief and moaning, "Ohhhhh, mercy."

"Uncle Versie, I'm surprised that you would react like this. You are much of a man, a man among men. Don't cry because Highball's dead. We got puppies from Highball. His sons and daughters will grow up to be as famous as Highball."

Uncle Versie said, "Shut your mouth, boy. I ain't cryin' 'cause the dog got killed. What upsets me is that old Highball is goin' to spend eternity thinkin' that coon killed him."

✉ Straight from the U.S. Mail Bag

I get a lot of really good mail from you folks out there. When I asked Tandy Rice in Nashville and Judy Moore in Yazoo City to just go ahead and pick some out for y'all to share, they came up with the following.

Dear Jerry:
All together now, let us conjugate the verb "am older."
I "am older!"
You "am older."
He, she or it "am older!"
We is all getting older.
Come to think of it, that's OK.
September 28 is a great time for a celebration of the event.

Best wishes,
Wilmer C. Fields, Vice-President
Executive Committee
Southern Baptist Convention

Editor's Note: Jerry's sixtieth birthday inspired the above.

27

Newgene and the Lion

I was down on Route 4 in Liberty, Mississippi, not long ago getting ready to leave when Uncle Versie said, "Jerry, there's just one more thing; I want you to talk to Newgene."

Newgene, you remember, was the meanest young'un whoever lived and the biggest liar I have ever known. I remember there was a big yellow collie dog in the community where I lived. Every year the man who owned that collie would take a set of sheep shears and shear that big old yellow long-haired collie dog. One summer he sheared that dog and left just a ring of hair around its neck and a great big bunch of hair around its tail. Newgene saw that dog and ran screaming into the house.

"Lion in the yard! Ohh, a lion's gonna get us. He's out in the backyard." Uncle Versie looked out and saw it was just that old collie dog, and he said, "Newgene, you go upstairs. I've told you about lying. I done beat you and I done whupped you, so you go up there and you pray. If you feel like the Lord has sufficiently let you know you are forgiven, then I won't whup you. But you go up there and pray thirty minutes about lying."

In a little while Newgene came down the steps, and Uncle Versie said, "Do you have peace in your heart that you have been forgiven for lying about that dog?"

"Yessir."

"Did the Lord make it real to you?"

"Yessir, the Lord spoke to me. The Lord told me first time he saw that dog, he thought it was a lion, too."

Just Merely Talking to God

P rayer is just merely talking to God, an expression of what's on your heart—how to do it, where to do it, when to do it, how often—I don't think it's all that complicated, but I think some folks misunderstand it.

Rev. Jim Yates, my preacher and pastor of the First Baptist Church of Yazoo City, Mississippi, and I were at a basketball game once. Brother Yates is a big Kentucky fan, and I am a big Mississippi State fan; we have had the privilege of going to the Southeastern Conference basketball tournaments together for a good long time. This particular occasion we were in Lexington, Kentucky. Alabama was playing Kentucky, and the winner would take the Southeastern Conference Championship.

Just before tipoff a Kentucky fan came running up to my preacher. She had seen him earlier that day on television with me, and she said, "Oh, Brother Jim, please pray that Kentucky wins this ball game." And Brother Jim replied, "Lady, I don't think God cares who wins this game."

Amen. I agree with the preacher. Now if she had asked for Kentucky to play without injury or to the best of its ability, that would have been OK, but to pray for a Kentucky win doesn't sit right. I don't think God intends for us to pray to Him on such subjects.

I heard a story about a baseball game where every time one of the players came up to bat he would make the sign of the cross before stepping into the batter's box. The third time he did this, an old bat boy sitting near a Catholic priest said, "Father, does his makin' the sign of the cross and prayin' like that cause him to hit the baseball better?" And the priest said, "If he can hit."

One time folks up in the Carolinas were having a special prayer meeting to bring rain; those folks needed rain bad. I mean it

Filming Ain't God Good *with Chuck Warren of Life Productions was a fine experience. I am really proud the film took top honors at New York's International Film Festival in the Ethics and Religion category.*

was a drought. They had called this special meeting to pray for rain. That's commendable. I believe in it. Had I been there I would have joined them; I would have petitioned God to send rain. That is a legitimate request for prayer.

This prayer meeting went on for about forty-five minutes, and one farmer sitting in the corner hadn't prayed. He wasn't paying much attention to the goings on and the pastor said, "Brother Floyd, I see you're not praying. Don't you want rain?"

"I want rain so bad I can taste it. Oooh, I need rain."

"Well, why aren't you joining in and praying for rain?"

"There ain't no need to pray for rain as long as the wind is out of the east."

Oh, ye of little faith! To have faith and to pray believing are essentials of prayer.

The most misunderstood ideas about prayer are those pertaining to prayer in the public schools. Lots of folks send me letters and stop me at airports wanting to talk about prayer in the public schools. Some argue that school prayer is communication with God and ought to be allowed under the First Amendment. In my opinion that approach misses the point altogether for a very simple reason; school prayer has never been forbidden in the first place. Period!

Now I understand why some people are confused and upset, because many things written about school prayer are erroneous. Some sincere folks have apparently been led to believe the Supreme Court outlawed prayer in schools. The Supreme Court did no such thing. My daughter, Katy Clower, is still in the public schools. All the time I say to her, "Katy, make sure today, darlin', that you put your head down during some quiet free time and say a brief prayer. Don't pray out loud; pray silently because you're praying to God, not to the students in your classroom."

I can't positively tell you what God will do about her prayer, but I'll tell you something that won't happen. No American Civil Liberties Union will come in and say the law is being violated. And they won't arrest anybody, and nobody will get any threatening letters from the Supreme Court. The only thing that could happen is that God could answer Katy's prayer—and ain't that wonderful!

Let me tell you something else that could happen to Katy. A teacher could show up at one of the classrooms and say, "Children, we're fixing to have a prayer. I'm doing this even though I represent the school system, but I want to say that Johnny and Mable don't have to join in this prayer because they're heathens and they're atheists."

What the teacher did is what the Supreme Court *has* outlawed, but Katy has religious freedom in the classroom now. Voluntary prayer has not been outlawed. All of us who are yelling about this ought to praise God the Supreme Court has kept folks from taking religious freedom away from our children in the classroom.

Now, what the Supreme Court did causes us parents to work harder as parents. We have to teach our children to want to pray, and we have to teach them prayer is something you do of your own free will rather than having some teacher put you through it like a geography lesson. And that is a wonderful thing. Hallelujah! Praise God from whom all blessings flow! Now let's bow our heads and pray.

Is Anybody There?

Newgene Ledbetter was driving a truck around a sharp curve. He lost control and dropped down about fifty feet, got tossed out of the truck but managed to hang on to one of those little persimmon sprouts. That was all there was between him and the drop-off below—looked about four thousand feet.

He started praying as hard as he could. He said, "Is anybody up there to listen to me? I need some help."

And a voice yelled down into the ravine, "Son, have faith and turn a-loose."

Newgene thought a second and then asked, "Is anybody else up there?"

66 Jerry Clower is so full of comedy, it's a wonder he doesn't explode. Well, I guess he does explode when he performs and it's a wonder. **99**

Roy Blount, Jr.
Author of *It Grows on You*
and other books of humor

Dope, Corn Silks, and High Limbs on a Sweet Gum

Cocaine, marijuana, crack, grapevine, and corn silks.

I'm a little more tolerant of people who get hooked on drugs than I used to be. And I'm going to tell you why. I've been working it out.

When I was coming up, we didn't have any money. One of the ways we entertained ourselves was rolling corn silk up in cigarette paper and smoking it. Or we would go to the woods and cut a grapevine and if we got it lit, we could suck smoke through the vine. It sure would make your tongue sore so I wasn't big on grapevines. But wanting "to be one of the boys" caused me to try them . . . corn silks and some rabbit tobaccer, too. Peer pressure's a powerful thing.

I remember one time I got to the swimming hole and old Lane was way up in the top of a sweet gum tree. And he yelled out, "Look, everybody, nobody ever in the history of the world has dived from this high limb into water that ain't but five feet deep. I'm the first one and I'm backing all y'all down."

Out of that tree he came and everybody started looking at me.

"Jerry, are you going to let Lane back you down?"

Well, Lane came up the bank out of the swimming hole about that time, spitting water and grinning and giggling, "Ha, ha, HA! Yea, yea, YEA, Jerry, I've done backed you down. I double-dog-dare you to dive out of that tree as high as I did."

My mind went to catching that school bus the next morning and I thought about how awkward it would be to hear everybody a-yelling, "Lane backed you dowwwwn. You were chiiiicken," and I just couldn't stand it. I climbed that sweet gum tree wanting to prove I wasn't scared to dive from as high as Lane. Not only was I not scared, I was going to dive from one limb higher! And I did. And I yelled. And out of the tree I came. I skint my belly up, but I assume to this day I hold the record of diving from the highest limb of that sweet gum tree.

Now as I look back on it, wasn't I stupid?! Anybody who would risk his life to keep people from saying, "I'll do something you won't do," is stupid. But that was the peer pressure of my day.

The peer pressure of today double-dares, "Here's some little stuff. I'll suck it up my nose. Why don't you suck it up yours?"

Hey, please, young people, listen to me. Do as Daniel in the Bible did. He was willing to stand alone. When the king ordered everybody to stop praying, everybody did except Daniel. People warned him, "Hey, Daniel, the king is going to throw you in the lion's den, and the lions are going to eat you up if you don't quit praying. You're supposed to be paying all your homage to the king, not to the Lord." But Daniel had a deep conviction and he shook his head and said, "I will not compromise."

Well, the king had him thrown into the lion's den, but the lion just purred and licked Daniel's hand and didn't do anything to him. The king sent for Daniel, and they talked. And Daniel said, "The Lord's weighed you and you don't weigh anything." And just about that time the door flew open and the enemy of the king came in and cut off the king's head.

Daniel had won. He stood alone against pressure to give up prayer, and he came out ahead. I beg young people when the pressure is on: do what's right even if you have to stand alone.

Yes, sir, I've been thinking about it. I said I've been growing more tolerant, too. And the how-come of that is a shocker.

Not too long ago I had the privilege of doing "Family Feud" on ABC television. I was part of a Country Music team with Bill Anderson, Larry Gatlin, Jeanne Pruitt, Ricky Skaggs, and Opry manager Hal Durham playing for the Grand Ole Opry Trust Fund. We opposed a western team working for one of the world hunger charities: Amanda Blake, Miss Kitty on "Gunsmoke"; Pat Buttram of the old "Gene Autry Show" and "Green Acres"; Doug McClure of "The Virginian"; Dale Robertson of "Wells Fargo"; and Dennis Weaver of "Gunsmoke" and "McCloud." We were having a great time—clowning around and having lots of laughs. I mean the mood was light, folks.

It was country vs. western at a special "Family Feud" taping. Opry members included myself, Bill Anderson, Jeanne Pruett, Larry Gatlin, Ricky Skaggs. Opry manager Hal Durham showed up to lend his support. On the right, opposing us were western stars Dennis Weaver, Amanda Blake, Pat Buttrum, Dale Robertson, and Doug McClure.

At one time our team had to come up with fruits that started with the letter *p*. Sound easy? Well, it is when you're at home all comfortable with your belly flopping over your unhooked belt. But we were sweating this one out. It meant $11,000 for the Grand Ole Opry Trust Fund. Ricky Skaggs, started off with "pear," an audience favorite, and, of course, we hit "peaches," but Larry Gatlin threw in "persimmon," and that old horn sounded; persimmon was not up on the big board, so it came down to me and everybody was yelling, "You can do it, Jerry." I squeezed my eyes shut and pictured that horn-of-plenty and what came rolling off my tongue was "pernanner."

We got so rambunctious between tapings the Hollywood folks wished we'd simmer down a bit, so Larry Gatlin and I began to fellowship. He's an old friend, a Christian, and whenever we get together we exchange something we've heard our preachers saying. In the course of conversation, I asked Larry what he was planning to do after these shows were taped. He said, "I'm going to check into the clinic down here and be treated for drugs."

I grabbed him by the shoulders and I said, "Larry, you and I clown and we cut up, but we don't joke about this. Don't you make any kind of joke about dope."

Tears started down his cheeks, and he looked me in the face and he said, "Jerry, I am addicted to cocaine."

I cannot describe my feelings. It was like someone had hit me between the eyes with an axe. Here was a young man who had grown up in a fundamental church, who had written, "The Light at the End of the Tunnel," and other beautiful songs. We have praised the Lord together many a time. And I thought, "If the devil can get Larry Gatlin to use cocaine, most anybody could get hooked on it."

Larry said he had tried just a little bit in the back of a limousine one time. He knew there was nothing to it, and he would never do it again, but wham! When people on television say cocaine is a big lie, believe it. I'm a lot more tolerant than I used to be. What's the answer? I don't know. I do believe we need more emphasis on catching the folks who sell it more than on those who use it. And I know if Larry Gatlin can get hooked, I feel a lot more tolerant toward those others who are hooked. I do know, too, and so does Larry now, that with proper treatment, you can remove the hook.

I'll tell you one thing: nobody ever gets hooked on dope who doesn't ever use any in the first place.

The Lord is not interested in what you used to do, but in what you're going to do from today on.

The Dog and the Bear

Newgene Ledbetter would climb a tree to get to tell a lie when he could stand on the ground and tell you the truth. I mean it got bad. The deacons and the pastor of his church decided to do something about it.

"Newgene's a great fella," they said, "but he just feels like he's got to lie all the time."

The preacher said, "Listen, let's go over to his house. Let's sit down and tell him the most bodacious, outlandish, damnable lie that's ever been told in the history of the world. We'll keep a straight face and tell it for the truth, and he'll see how ridiculous it is for good people to lie and maybe he'll stop lying."

The deacons said, "All right, preacher, who's going to be the spokesman?"

Preacher said, "I am."

They knocked on the door of Newgene's house and Newgene let them in.

"Glad to see you. Set down."

Preacher said, "Newgene, would you believe that last Lord's Day while I was preaching, the spirit of the Lord was moving the back door of the church open, and down the aisle of the church came a huge, vicious brindle-colored grizzly bear and right behind him, chasing him was a little old bitty black and white dog. That bear squatted right by the Lord's supper table, right in front of the pulpit and that little bitty dog jumped on him and they commenced to fighting. They wallowed down the first eight rows of pews in the church. Women were fainting. Hair was flying. You ain't never seen or heard such a terrible fight. When the fur quit flying, that little old dog had completely whupped that vicious, brindle-colored grizzly bear and not only whupped him but consumed him. Now, Newgene, do you believe that?"

Newgene said, "Heck, yeah, I believe that. That was my dog."

Happiest Moments of My Life

I'm often asked by talk-show interviewers, "What was the happiest moment of your life," and I tell them, "The day when, at thirteen, I publicly professed my faith in Christ." I feel sometimes they wish I would answer differently, but I have to be truthful, so they keep asking and I keep telling.

One hot July day in 1939 my mama told my brother, Sonny, and me, "Now, boys, y'all stop plowing a little early today because tomorrow is the fourth Sunday in July and the East Fork Baptist Church is having a revival meeting." The East Fork Baptist Church was organized in 1810, and it has been having a revival week every year since then.

One of the real highlights of my life was to go back to the one hundred seventy-fifth anniversary of that old church, but the happiest moment of my life was Thursday night, following the fourth Sunday in July of 1939. I really understood what the preacher was saying when he told of God's plan of salvation. At the end of the service, with the congregation singing "Only Trust Him," I walked down that aisle and experienced a grace that comes only from the saving power of God. That same night a little thirteen-year-old girl publicly professed her faith in Christ and followed me down the aisle. Her name was Homerline Wells, now the mother of my four children, and I some kinda' love her. We have been married *happily* over forty years. The happiest moment in my life was when I became a Christian.

Now when those interviewers want to know about the next happiest moment, I tell them about being in the Navy. I joined the Navy at seventeen, the day after I finished high school. I went to boot camp at Camp Perry, Virginia, then to radio school at Miami University, Oxford, Ohio, and I ended up a radio operator in the

South Pacific on the USS *Bennington*, an aircraft carrier. One day on watch I was monitoring a voice channel between the *Bennington* and the airplanes flying off the ship. We had launched a squadron of planes toward their target when an officer aboard the USS *Bennington* got on the radio and said, "Hello, this is Jocko. (Jocko was the code-voice name of the *Bennington*.) The Potsdam Proclamation will be forthcoming soon. Drop bombs well clear of target and return to base."

Well, my heart stopped beating for a few minutes. The war was over. The Potsdam Proclamation meant the Japanese had surrendered, and we weren't going to have to worry about being bombed or killed any more. Well, needless to say, the radio circuit was mighty busy. Folks were talking and hollering and screaming. I was trying to type it down as best I could, and I remember one of the airplanes gave an emergency signal indicating that everybody should listen.

"Hello, Jocko, this is Jocko 115." (He was the number 115 airplane operating off the ship.) And this deep Southern voice said as seriously as you could say anything, "Has the Governor of Texas been informed about the terms of this peace treaty?" The pilot acted as if he were as serious as could be, and he wanted the officer aboard the ship to check with the Governor of Texas to see if the

Jeanne Pruett and I were both inducted into the Opry in 1973. (Photo by Melodie Gimple)

peace terms were agreeable to the Governor. The end of that war was my second happiest moment.

The icing on the cake—the third happiest moment of my life—occurred the night I was inducted into the Grand Ole Opry. When I was a little boy we used to pray that we would clear enough money at the end of the crop year to go see WSM's Grand Ole Opry in Nashville, Tennessee. Well, we never did make it. The first time I ever *saw* the Opry I *performed* on it as a special guest. Then in 1973 I was invited to become a regular member.

About forty people came up from Mississippi for the induction ceremony. Sitting in the front row was Governor Bill Waller of Mississippi; the mayor of Yazoo City; Homerline; my mama; my brother and his wife, Jody; Chief Hill and Margarita, my next door neighbors; and all of my children. Katy was a little bitty thing then, wanting to dance on the edge of the stage, wanting to see Porter Wagoner.

Mr. Roy Acuff picked up Katy and gave her a hug. It was just beautiful. I was pretty emotional and I knew my mama was. I could see tears on the cheeks of most everybody in the front row, so I was hoping Mama could keep her composure and not go to wailing when they brought her up on stage. Jody was squalling uncontrollably; emotion had really taken a-hold of her. Mama had witnessed it all and I was praying, "Oh, God, please let my mama bear up under this emotional moment. Everybody got really quiet when Mama came up to me on stage. She put out her hand and sort of rubbed the side of my face softly, looking up at me, and she said, "Baby, what is a Goo Goo?" (The Goo Goo people heard about that later and sent her a gross—one dozen dozen, 144 clusters!)

I shouldn't have worried about Mama on that happy day.

Dove Hunter

One September, an old Nashville buddy of mine, Mr. Don Fowler, told me he was coming to Yazoo City and wanted to do some dove hunting.

"We'll be glad to have you," I told him.

He arrived and we got out in one of those soybean patches fixing to thump some of those turtle doves. Now they're delicious. You take the breast of that dove, put a gob of butter into the chest cavity of that dove and then wrap a piece of raw bacon around it, fastening it with a toothpick, and lay it side-down on a charcoal grill. Ooowee, is that good. It will make a puppy pull a freight train!

We were squatting down under a cypress tree getting ready for those doves. Directly two doves came flying across the field and right up in midair they just stopped and fell down to the ground.

I said, "Did you hear a gun shooting?"

"No, I didn't."

"Well, what killed those doves?" I said. "I didn't even see any smoke."

About that time a couple more doves got right up over the center of the field and just stopped dead in the air and fell—whoom—to the ground.

"Let's go check on this," I said.

We gathered up our guns and started out to the center of the field. Right there in the center we found an old boy I know from Yazoo City, Peter Plug. He was hunkered down with his head turned up toward the heavens like a goose getting a drink of water while it's raining.

"Peter Plug, what are you doing?"

He said, "I'm grinning these doves to death."

"You what?"

"It's a gift I have and if you can put that ugly grin on your face and look 'em right in the eye, wham! Down they come."

"Peter, do you know of anybody else who has this gift?"

"My wife can do it a heap better than I can. She can really ugly-grin 'em down."

"Well, do you ever bring her hunting with you?"

"Heck, no. She tears 'em up too bad."

✉ Straight from the U.S. Mail Bag

Memo to JAYREE
From   Tandy Rice

Re: What do Prince, Diana Ross, and Jerry Clower have in common?

We've been contacted today by Paul Brown, Program Director of WVOI, a black radio station in Toledo, Ohio. About three months ago he went into an R & B record store to acquire more humor material, and the only thing on hand was an album by you, a white man from the South of whom Brown had never heard.

He bought the album, started playing a cut each day and said the response was fantastic. Many of his black listeners were calling in asking for more, saying, "He reminds me of my grandfather back home."

Brown suspended Clower air play for a week to test the market and validate what he thought he was hearing from his audience; the switchboard lit up in protest. The station's latest ratings' book shows it has jumped to Number Three in the market, and Brown attributes most of that success of Jerry Clower.

Saddest Moments of My Life

A lot of people right off think I will name the loss of a loved one as the saddest moment of my life. But all the loved ones I've ever lost were Christians and their deaths were home-going events.

Certainly it was a sad night for me when I was called to the scene of a wreck where folks thought my boy was dead because they couldn't wake him up. But I leaned on my Christian faith and I prayed hard, "Lord, whatever happens, let me praise your holy name." We had some sad days at the hospital until his head injury cleared up, but he ended up being perfectly normal.

As I think about what really was the saddest moment in my life, the one that keeps coming back to my mind occurred the day I was driving from Baton Rouge, Louisiana, years ago to Yazoo City, Mississippi. I was coming by Southwest Mississippi to visit Mama. I had been to Baton Rouge because every year Louisiana State University puts on a conference there concerning the proper ways to apply anhydrous ammonia as a nitrogen product and how to handle it safely in order to grow good crops.

I left LSU feeling real happy about that conference, just driving up the old plank road and listening to some country music. Just before I hit Highway 48 a voice came over the Baton Rouge radio station and said, "Ladies and gentlemen, the President of the United States has been shot in Dallas, Texas. Details will follow in a moment."

Well, I said, "Oh, Lord, I fought a war to give us the right to have a democracy in the United States of America and here's our Number One leader, wounded and in trouble. Somebody is sick enough to try to kill him." I felt numb all over.

I left the radio on and kept driving toward my mama's house. An announcer explained that a sniper had shot President John F. Kennedy who was in the hospital, and Vice President Lyndon Johnson was standing by. Then the saddest moment hit when a voice from the network interrupted, "Ladies and gentlemen, the President of the United States is dead." I pulled over to the side of the road and wept. There I was, two-hundred-seventy pounds, six-feet tall, former football player for Mississippi State, former fighting man on an aircraft carrier in the Southwest Pacific, sitting there beside the road crying. It broke my heart that our society could produce somebody who would take that drastic action to express his views against the government. I believe the day that President Kennedy was shot could be the saddest day of my life.

It was a sad day when James Meredith enrolled at the University of Mississippi, and the leadership of the state did not encourage everybody to cool it. A bunch of folks went to Oxford and confronted several thousand troops, spending several million dollars to put a student in the University of Mississippi. I listened to the broadcasts telling about fires on campus and the death of two people, and the suffering of more. I remember getting down on my knees in my bedroom and praying, "Oh, dear God, if my attitude has caused some people to react to this situation like this, I hereby re-dedicate my life. I'm going to change, because I don't want to encourage an attitude that would cause people to break the law, kill folks, or keep a qualified student from entering the University of Mississippi."

Gathering Votes

Clovis Ledbetter got himself a job as a deputy sheriff working right on the line between Mississippi and Louisiana. Now this individual sheriff's department was notorious for gathering the names of the dead when an election time rolled around if the sheriff didn't have sufficient votes to get elected.

The night before the election the sheriff and his deputy sheriff, Clovis Ledbetter, were out in the graveyard with their clipboards writing down names. They started on the far side and got right in the middle of the graveyard when the sheriff told Clovis, "We can stop now. We got enough names. This is sufficient. Let's go." Clovis said, "Nah-aw, no you don't. We ain't going to be unfair about this thing. I tell you right now we're gonna write down every name in this graveyard because these people over here on this side's got just as much right to vote as those folks over there."

I hope and pray that we get this sectionalism done away with as far as America is concerned. I don't want folks to sell their birthright or lose their heritage, but I want America to be one great big country, and everybody as Americans, and everybody loving one another and getting it on.

45

Things I Hope Never Happen Again

I travel two hundred days a year. People say, "Jerry, how can you stand to travel so much?" Well, I look at traveling as part of my job.

But as I travel, I run into some things that make me think, "One day I'll hang this up and I'll never get into this situation again."

I hope I never again sit down in a restaurant to eat breakfast and be faced with a little doodad of jelly. You've got to have a fingernail like you see advertised on television or a magnifying glass to get into it. You finally figure out what corner to slip your fingernail under, and you squeeze the doodad half in two pulling it open. Some restaurants have the good sense to put a jam jar on the table;

B. J. Thomas wears a cross on his chain. I wear a cross and a Star of David because I believe what the Bible says about both of them. The inscription on the picture B. J. sent me reads, "I know we'll always be happy if we keep our eyes on the cross."

you can just raise the lid, pick up a spoon and dip up a gob of jelly. That's great. (Butter comes in those little doodads, too. I'd rather cut me a slice of butter or spoon a gob from a crock than mess with one of those doodads any day.)

I hope I never again walk up to the desk of a motel or a hotel and get defeated by an invisible reserver. Just as the desk clerk reaches for papers for you to sign, the phone rings, and while you're ready to tend to business with money in your pocket, that clerk will start discussing room rates for a reservation four months off. That's planned inefficiency.

"Will you hold please? I have a cash payin' customer here, live and ready to go to his room," that clerk should say. "Hold on just a minute, and as soon as I do business with this live man with cash money in his pocket, then me and you'll talk about a reservation four months from now."

Sometimes at the very best hotels in the world, I'll go to my room, put the key in the door, and—whooee—the room is already occupied. That is the most embarrassing thing that could possibly happen. Recently, I checked into one of the fanciest hotels in the country. The bellman was busy, so I said, "That's all right. I'll just go on up to my room." I put the key in the door and walked in on a couple. Now not only is this embarrassing, but it can also get you killed. I don't see why the clerk can't have some kind of alarm siren that screeches if he's fixing to put somebody in a room and there's already somebody in it, or maybe a big fireworks display going off, or three or four flags unfurling, or something. There ought to be a way to avoid that happening to anybody again, much less me.

I was in an airport restaurant the other day and encountered a long line just to check out at the register. Up at the head of the line was a fellow putting a $1.97 breakfast on a credit card. Fifteen people were standing in line. The poor cashier was on the telephone trying to see if his credit card was good. If you haven't got enough

Regardless of your occupation, whether you drive a truck, dig a ditch, milk a cow, sweep a street, or haul garbage, if you're doing that job to the best of your ability, then you are successful. If you're not giving an honest day's work for an honest day's pay, then you ain't successful.

money to buy breakfast and not make me stand in line behind you, stay at home.

Sometimes I enter a restaurant and the hostess will walk toward me with a menu in her hand saying, "Do you want something?" I wanna say, "No, I've just come down here to see you."

Why don't they just say, "One for breakfast, one for lunch or one for supper"? Just don't say, "May I help ya?" Certainly she can help me. I wouldn't be there if she couldn't.

Cold grits. They bring your eggs over light and your sausage, and the grits are so cold they've gotten hard and congealed—like they came out of the refrigerator. I hope I never have to put up with that again.

I hope I never again have to put up with folks trying to change my culture. I stopped at a restaurant in the Memphis airport not long ago and ordered my breakfast: "Two eggs over light, sausage, whole wheat toast or biscuit if you got 'em, and grits." In a determined, loud voice, the attendant said, "We don't serve grits; we have hash browns." "Lady," I said, "I growed up poor. But I never was so poor I had to eat a hash potato for breakfast."

"Do you want to see the manager?"

"Darlin', I ain't being ugly. I ain't aggravated at you. You're just doing your job, but I would, in a spirit of love, like to ask the manager why, in a Southern town, they are tryin' to take grits away from us."

Well, the manager came out and said, "We just don't have 'em; we did away with 'em."

I said, "Well, darlin', W. C. Handy is buried over yonder on the Mississippi River. He may tear out of the ground and kill all of y'all."

A country radio station interviewed me that afternoon, and I brought it up. Ninety-nine percent of the people who called in said, "Do not take grits away from us. They're a part of our Southern culture."

I did the show that night in Memphis, Tennessee. The mayor of the town came backstage and bragged to me, "Jerry, whenever we have industrialists come to Memphis we don't have big dinners for them, we have breakfasts and serve them grits."

I said, "Well, don't take them to the airport restaurant then,

Russell Reeves (left) and David Morris (right), editor of Game and Fish, *and I try quail hunting in Georgia.*

they don't serve grits out there." And this mayor, a typical Southern traditionalist, threw a fit. Anything good in the way of tradition, he wanted to keep.

The folks who own that big chain restaurant wrote me a letter and apologized. "There will be grits in this restaurant just as long as this is still the South," they promised.

On the bright side, grits can sometimes be found up North. I was doing a theater-in-the-round at Cleveland, Ohio, with Loretta Lynn. We went out after the show to a Denny's Restaurant and ordered breakfast.

"Do you want grits or hash browns," the waitress said.

I just jumped up and hugged her.

" How long has your husband been an entertainer?" asked a reporter.

"I've known Jerry Clower since I was thirteen years old, and I've never seen a day when he wasn't entertaining somebody. **"**

Homerline Clower

Tar Baby

I remember a lady who lived in Amite County near a construction site, and workers were putting a tar roof on the building near her house. This lady had sixteen young'uns—one every year—just like a brood sow.

One day she lost one of her children. She got to hunting him and, come to find out, he had fallen into a fifty-gallon drum of that black roofing tar at the construction site. She reached down, hauled him up, took a look at him and shoved him back down in that drum of tar. She said, "Boy, it'd be a lot easier to have another one than to clean you up."

Brenda Lee and I greet each other at Fan Fair, 1986. (Photo by Beth Gwinn)

Happy Homes and a Dinner of Herbs

It seems to me war has been declared on family life. Families are racked by divorce, confusion in parental roles, a breakdown in authority, the absence of one or both parents, money troubles, and a host of other problems. Do we need a guidebook to show us how to have happy homes? Yes. And I am happy to announce we have one. The guidebook is the Bible. Right there we can find an outline for good family relationships; we need to take seriously the Word of God on how to do this.

Years ago, I was on the road selling fertilizer. Passing through Baton Rouge, Louisiana, I saw a great big billboard announcing, "Happy Homes for Sale, three bedrooms, two baths, and a den." Well, that's misleading.

You can buy a house, but folks have got to occupy that house in order to have a happy home. My wife and I have been happily married for forty years. I first put my eyes on her in church. We are actively engaged in church, and most of our social activities go on in the church, so I think happy homes start through the local church. Happy homes will never be happy if one or more family members are negative all the time, nitpicking and griping. I've read several times, "Marriage is a fifty-fifty proposition." What a lie. Sometimes it's more like ninety/ten and *you're* going to be the ten *some of the time* and somebody else is going to be the ninety.

Love is the key word for a happy home. I'm not talking about puppy love, little sugar dripping, do-dinky love. I'm talking about sure 'nuf love. When I was a boy, for a while there were just three of us in the family: my mama, my brother, Sonny, and me. Sometimes we'd run down a fine-sized chicken, wring its neck, douse it in a kettle of hot, scalding water, and we'd stand in the yard picking all the feathers off that chicken. We would be motivated to prepare ourselves for a good fried chicken dinner. When we sat down to eat that chicken, my mama would always say, "Boys, give me that

Homerline and I love to spend time with our grandsons, Jayree, who is Billy and Amy Clower Elmore's son, and Wesley Burns Clower, who is named for his great-great grandfather and is the son of Ray and Nan Clower.

back and the neck, and the feet. The back of that chicken is my favorite piece." My brother and I would eat that pulley bone, breasts, thighs and, drumsticks; I'd get the gizzard, my favorite piece. I actually thought my mama really liked chicken backs and feet and necks until I got old enough to realize what was happening. My mama so loved me and my brother she wanted us to have the good pieces of chicken. That's the kind of love I'm talking about.

Not long ago my grandson, Jayree, was spending some time with me and his grandmother. Jayree had toys scattered all over the den floor. My wife, Homerline, said, "Jayree, pick up these toys, son, and stack them over yonder somewhere. Folks can't even walk through the den. Somebody's gonna trip over that stuff and hurt himself."

Well, he just kept fumbling with those toys and pushing them around, not paying any attention to what he was told.

Directly my wife said, "Jayree, did you hear me? I said to pick up the toys."

Homerline and I celebrated the wedding of our daughter Sue to Ken Hall, Youth Director of the First Baptist Church of Yazoo City, in December, 1986. Ken's youth group organized a choir to perform specially selected music. (Photo by Sidney Aust)

Jayree put his hands on his hips, looked at me and said, "Grandaddy, how have you lived with her all these years?"

And it was a joy to sit the little fellow down and tell him how happy his grandmother and I had been for years and how we had told his mother to pick up toys in just the same tone of voice we had told him.

Now some folks make it a little more simple than it is. They'll go through this role of playing happy home saying, "God is going to take care of me." I tell a story on one of my records about an old boy who got caught in a flood. He got up on the top of his house, and the Civil Defense boat came pulling up to the house and the fellow on board said, "Sir, it's been predicted that the dam's gonna bust and if it busts, water will come up over your house. Get in this boat and let us rescue you."

"You go on and help somebody else. God's going to take care of me."

54

Well, in about thirty minutes the boat came back and this old boy had moved right up on the tip-top of the house. I mean there wasn't but about three inches of roof left. And the Civil Defense man said, "Sir, I'm warnin' you now, you'd better get in this boat and let us rescue you."

And the roof-sitter said, "You go on. God's going to take care of me."

In about an hour, the Civil Defense man showed up in a helicopter, and he looked down out of the window of the helicopter and there was that old boy standing up on top of the chimney, water completely covering his house, nothing sticking out but the chimney. That helicopter hovered down over him, lowered a rope, and a man with a bullhorn said, "Catch hold of the rope. This is your last chance. Let us rescue you. The dam has busted."

"Y'all go on," the old boy yelled. "God's going to take care of me."

Well, the fact is, the man drowned, graveyard dead. When he got to heaven, he told the Lord, "Lord, you let me down. I'm so disappointed. I told all them people that I had the faith that you was goin' to take care of me."

"You dummy," the Lord said. "I sent you two boats and a helicopter."

The key to a happy home is using the Bible as a guideline and really letting love take over. King Solomon said that it's better to eat poke salat or turnip greens, drink branch water out of a gourd dipper and live in a shotgun house full of love than it is to live in a mansion dining on rib-eye steaks three times a day and driving a great big old car—all without love. You don't believe King Solomon said that? Check the Book of Proverbs. "Better is a dinner of herbs where love is, Than a fatted calf with hatred." I just told you in East-Fork-Mississippi language what that verse means.

Letter from Home

I grew up on a farm and joined the 4-H Club at age nine. I wanted to grow up to be like the 4-H agent in my county because he so impressed me when I was a little boy. I worked my way through Mississippi State University, got a degree in agriculture, and the first job I ever had was as an assistant county agent in charge of 4-H Club work.

As a youngster in 4-H, I pledged "my head to clearer thinking, my heart to greater loyalty, my hands to larger service, my health to better living for my club, my community, my country, and my world." At Mississippi State University, I learned the Future Farmers of America motto: learning to do, doing to learn, earning to live, and living to serve.

I want to salute the American farmer. He does his job better than anybody else. Let's face it, automobile dealers have problems with competition from other countries; the computer people have

I love my fans. Here I am taking a break from signing autographs at Fan Fair in Nashville.

problems competing with other countries; but if people in other countries want to find out how to farm, they come to America. The American farmer has made so many adjustments to help himself.

Where I grew up, we didn't have electricity. You tell your young'uns when they complain about getting homework done you saw ole Jerry Clower, and he said he never got homework done in his life from the first through the twelfth grade other than by the light of a fireplace or a coal-oil lamp. That's the gospel truth. I was nineteen years old before I ever had electricity in my house, and I didn't witness it then; I was in Iwo Jima. I remember opening a letter from home, reading the news and running down the sands of Iwo Jima waving that thing over my head, screaming.

Those folks took to me, especially the Yankees. They said, "Rebel, you got a letter from home. What's the good news?"

I said, "Man, the REA has done throwed off a creosote pole in our front yard."

66 What was it like growing up with Jerry Clower? My father's success really got started when I was living in Germany where my husband was stationed in the army. I grew up with the fertilizer salesman from Yazoo City. Dad traveled a lot while I was growing up, but he always managed to be there when his children needed him. He has stood by me and given his support through good and bad times. I always knew I could turn to him.

He always set a Christian example for us to follow. My father has always been very outgoing and loved to be the center of attention. No matter where he was or what he was talking about, he always seemed to bring a little joy and laughter into people's lives. This is one characteristic about my father that I love and admire dearly.

What was it like growing up with Jerry Clower? I guess it was like growing up with any other father; however, my father is a very special, loving person whom I love very much. I am very fortunate and thankful to God for Jerry Clower, my father. 99

Amy Clower Elmore

Two Burnt Ears

I haven't told you much about old Ben DeLaughter. Old Ben was kind of trifling. All Ben wanted to do was dip snuff and let somebody make him a living, but when he fell in love he changed his mind. Ben got a job on the pipeline and worked hard enough to be put in one of those company houses at the pumping station. Old Ben was doing well and had a television set. He never had one before. One day he ran out of the house screaming and hollering and running to the company doctor's office. The doctor looked at him and asked, "My soul, Ben, what's the matter?"

Ben had two badly burned ears.

"Good gracious, Ben, let me put some salve on those ears. How in the world did you do this?"

Ben said, "This is my day off from work, and my wife and I were watching TV while she did the ironing. I'm on twenty-four-hour call in case they need me at the pumping station, and so I put the telephone right on the end of the ironing board to be handy. Doc, they done shot Ben Cartwright and I was so upset when that phone rang, I popped the hot iron to my ear. It buggered me up bad."

"Well, Ben, I don't believe I understand. How did you get the other ear burned?"

"Doc," he said, "Would you believe that dad-blamed phone rang again?"

Ego and Attitude

Show me a person who doesn't have an ego, and I'll show you an individual who is subdued, unhappy, or purposeless. Make your ego work *for* you by having the right kind of attitude. You may be shocked, but in certain instances, attitude is more important than facts. That's right, in some situations, your attitude about a matter is more important than the facts about the matter. David never would have fought Goliath had he listened to the facts.

I want to tell you something about the changing of my attitude. You know I went to Mississippi State University and got a degree in agriculture. Not too long afterwards, I started selling fertilizer, and I was good at it. I could send sacks of it to you by the truckload or boxcar. I had a tangible product to sell.

The day I backed into show business, all I had to sell was me, Jerry Clower, so I'm sure I came on a little too strong. It was through the guidance of my friend and manager, Tandy Rice, I began to change my attitude. Tandy said, "You don't have to be this ferocious in selling yourself." Well, I guess I had been ferocious, enthusiastic, egotistical. What had worked in selling tons of tangible product had to be toned down for selling just pounds of me.

I wanted to do my new job better than anybody else. Folks backstage at the Grand Ole Opry would say to me, "Jerry, how are you?" and I would say, "I'm fixin' to go out there and knock 'em dead," and I had myself believing that. But you gotta temper your ego with love. Love plays a part in everything.

I remember a story about two Christian businessmen having lunch in a downtown restaurant. A waitress, serving their table dumped a bowl of hot soup right over one of these businessmen. Well, everybody gasped and stared. They just couldn't wait for the manager to run out and fire this lady. They just couldn't wait for this man, standing there, dripping, with his suit ruined, to cuss

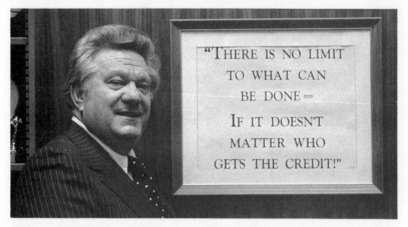

Years ago a pharmacist in McComb, Mississippi, removed this sign from the wall of his drugstore and gave it to me when I admired its philosophy. It's been hanging in my office ever since.

this waitress out, but the fellow looked at that waitress and said, "Young lady, I'm so sorry this happened to you. I know it embarrasses you."

Whew, what would you have done, Mr. Businessman? How would you have reacted to this situation? Would your ego allow you the attitude this fine man had?

✧ ✧ ✧

It bothers me sometimes when some folks serving the Lord feel they have to get it announced to every hedge and byroad in the world that they are active servants for the Lord. Now Gideons International gives the best illustration of proper attitude, enthusiasm, and ego. They have but one objective—to win men and women, boys and girls, to the Lord Jesus Christ. They are best known for placing Bibles all over the world.

In 1898, a man named John Nicholson entered the Central Hotel of Boscobel, Wisconsin, for the night. The hotel was full and the manager didn't know how to take care of his long-time friend and wonderful customer, but finally he decided to ask John Nicholson to share a room with another man. The manager told John, "This Sam Hill is a good clean fellow, and if it's agreeable with you, I'll put you both together in Room No. 19."

When they got ready to retire, Mr. Nicholson reached into his suitcase, got out a Bible and said to Mr. Hill, "I always read from God's Word and have a little talk with the Lord before I go to bed."

Mr. Hill replied, "Let me join in your devotions because I'm a Christian, and I'll enjoy having devotions with you." That night as they talked, they planned to organize a Christian businessmen's association with periodic devotional meetings designed to serve travelers.

Out of that meeting, the Gideons International had its birth. You never see Gideons seeking publicity. They simply believe what the Bible says, "My word . . . shall not return to Me void." That's what the Lord said. The Bible also says, "The grass withers, the flower fades, . . . But the word of our God stands forever."

Millions of copies of the Word of God have been placed all over the world with faith that it shall not return unto Him void.

It was my privilege and joy to serve on the International Cabinet of the Gideons International during the mid-fifties. I found out firsthand how ego and attitude ought to be applied to everyday living.

The most important business I'm engaged in ought to be the Lord's business. If it ain't, I need to get off and classify myself and see whose side I'm on.

The Clumsy Mule

Everybody always asks me why Uncle Versie Ledbetter and his wife got along so well. They never had an argument. On their fiftieth wedding anniversary they both testified they had never had a problem.

Now I heard a story about that. Back when Uncle Versie married Aunt Pet, he took the mule and the buggy, picked her up and carried her off to the church and married her. As they were driving home to their little shack, Uncle Versie was sitting in the buggy and had his arm up along the back of the buggy seat saying sweet things to Aunt Pet.

About that time the mule stumbled. Uncle Versie said, "That's number one." And then he turned and talked some more to Aunt Pet. Then in a little bit the mule stumbled again. He said, "That's number two," and he turned and talked to Aunt Pet. A little bit farther along the mule stumbled again, and Uncle Versie said, "All right, whoa! That's number three." He got his pistol, put it up to the mule's head, and killed him dead.

Aunt Pet said, "Versie, what in the world are you doing? What's wrong with you?"

He said, "That's number one!"

TV Preachers and the Slipping Foot

People keep asking me, "Jerry, what do you think about those TV preachers?" Then I hear *their* opinions and they usually act as if they are glad if a TV preacher is having problems. Now for a person who knows nothing about the Lord, this behavior doesn't surprise me. But for an individual who claims to be a follower of the Lord to joke and act happy because a TV preacher's having problems bothers me.

I remember when I was a student at Southwest Mississippi Junior College, I hadn't been married but a month or two when my wife and I visited her mama and daddy. We went to the East Fork Baptist Church right near where we were raised. Afterwards, I was standing in the kitchen where my mother-in-law was making biscuits. She had her little stubby hands in hog lard, blending it into flour, and she had poured some buttermilk over it so the squashing was getting good. She was fixing to work that dough up into pretty brown cathead biscuits. You bite into one of them and it's so good it would make a puppy pull a freight train.

Well, I was strutting back and forth across the kitchen complaining about the sermon we had heard. I had just turned twenty-one and I knew everything. I was telling my mother-in-law just how that preacher should have done his sermon. She wrung her hands together and let the dough fall down into the old dough tray; then she turned and pointed one of her stubby little flour-covered fingers at me saying, "Boy, be careful. You may be talkin' about God's anointed."

My, that struck me hard! I said, "Well, you know, if I'm talking about God's anointed, I had better be careful because God may get fed up with me talking about His anointed, and if He doesn't like me doing it, it wouldn't be too difficult for Him to shut me up."

My fondness for sports and sports figures is well-known. It would be hard to say who was more pleased by these meetings with Kansas City Royals' manager Dick Howser (left) and Royals' third baseman George Brett.

This godly lady replied, "It would be about as difficult for God to shut you up as it would be for the Panama Limited train doing one hundred miles an hour to knock a blade of Johnson grass off the railroad track."

From that day to this very moment, I have been very careful how I criticize any kind of individual who says he is a follower of God.

Now, it's no secret my first place of Christian service is in the local church. A friend told me the other day, "Jerry, I'm a tither, but I'm not a storehouse tither. I send some of my tithes to a preacher I'm helping up in the eastern part of the United States."

"Well," I said, "that's all right with me. I am a free moral agent under God, an autonomous human being. I belong to a church that is autonomous. We don't have to abide by anything except what our congregation meets and discusses and says we ought to do, and I believe in putting that local church first. If you feel good about what you're doing, go ahead; I just don't agree with you."

It wasn't long before my friend called and said, "My wife's going into the hospital, and I want you to pray for her."

"I'll be glad to. The Bible instructs us to bear one another's burdens, and I want to help you bear yours."

"I'm also going to call the pastor and tell him," he said.

Then I did an ugly thing. I said, "Friend, why don't you call that TV preacher you have been sending money to up yonder in the East?"

There was quiet on the telephone. He said, "Jerry, you're being pretty rough."

I said, "You ought to give your tithe to the storehouse and then over and above your tithe you ought to send it to that preacher."

I think sometimes we look into the face of the TV preacher—that good-looking, flamboyant, hair-sprayed, articulate communicator—when we ought to be looking into the face of Jesus. So if the TV preacher's foot slips, we not only will have the right attitude about forgiving him but we'll also know that we are looking into the face of Jesus, not into the face of the TV preacher representing Jesus.

66 I guess I've known Jerry about as long as anybody in the business. We go back to when Jerry made his first record, the one Grant Turner and John McDonald debuted on their noontime farm show. Jerry's a good friend; he always has been. I think the world of him. He's a great entertainer but most important, he's a great communicator, not only at the Grand Ole Opry but at church or selling fertilizer or whatever he happens to be doing. **99**

Hairl Hensley
Grand Ole Opry announcer and
WSM radio host

My Katy Burns

K aty Burns sneaked up on Homerline and me. My wife was forty-four years old when Katy was born. My little Katy Burns was driving with me in my new Dodge pickup truck one time playing grown-up. Five-years old then, she was lying on the floor of that truck pulling off a little pair of white gloves she had on her hands. All of a sudden she screamed; I thought she'd been stung by a wasp. "Ohhh, Daddy, Daddy, Daddy." I said, "Darlin', what is the matter?" She said, "Daddy, if I had one more finger I could count to eleven."

66 I have known Jerry for more than thirty years and shared many memorable times with him. In 1977 President Jimmy Carter came to Yazoo City, Mississippi, to hold one of his town meetings. Two weeks later my wife, Juanita, and I were in Nashville, Tennessee, to see the Grand Ole Opry. As Jerry's guests, we were visiting backstage at the Opry when all of a sudden men dressed in business suits and carrying walkie-talkies surrounded the stage area. Jerry got real excited when he learned what was happening. Vice-President Mondale was making an appearance at the Opry and Jerry had been asked to introduce him. Jerry walked stage center with Vice-President Mondale and roared into the mike over national TV, "Whooeee, shoot this thing." With all those secret service men around, Jerry is the only one who could say such a thing and get away with it. Jerry, the grand host, introduced my wife and me to Vice-President Mondale—a memorable event in our lives. **99**

Charles E. Fulgham
Mayor, Yazoo City, Mississippi

Doing the Best with What You Got

Please know, I am for education. I believe in it. In fact, I got the best education offered in America. Had it not been for public education, I couldn't read or write, because we didn't have money to get any kind of education except that offered by the public schools. But it bothers me a little bit when I hear people proclaiming that education alone will straighten out America.

A lot of people today enjoy criticizing educators. "Why can't Johnny read?" they ask. Well, usually the reason why Johnny can't read is that he doesn't give a dad-blame whether he can read or not; he's not motivated. Johnny ought to be able to read. It's tragic that he can't read, but he needs to do the best he can with what he's got. That's motivation that can lead to all kinds of success.

Take Uncle Versie Ledbetter. Uncle Versie could just barely read and write because he had very little schooling, but he did the best he could with what he had. He was motivated! Uncle Versie was Marcel Ledbetter's daddy and we loved him. One day we followed Uncle Versie to town wondering what in the world he was going to do there. Well, he slipped into the bank and we eased around and watched him walk up to one of the windows occupied by a woman teller. Uncle Versie and this woman chatted a while and she pointed to a man sitting behind a big desk across the room. Uncle Versie proceeded to sit down in a chair across from that important gentleman, and that well-dressed banker said, "Mr. Ledbetter, what can I do for you?"

"I want to borrow some money."

"What do you have to put up?"

"A $10,000-matured savings bond."

The banker smiled and said, "I'll loan you any amount you want up to $10,000." (That was real generous of that banker, wasn't it?)

"I wanna' borrow a dollar," Uncle Versie said.

"My good man, we just don't loan a dollar."

"Then you lied to me! You said you'd loan any amount up to $10,000."

"You're right," the banker admitted. "I did say that, and I am going to honor my word. Here's a dollar. Sign this note right here for a year. Give me that savings bond as collateral, and I'll see you in a year."

Uncle Versie went back to the bank in a year, walked up to the banker and popped a dollar down on the desk and said, "There's the dollar that I owe you. I wanna' pay off that note. How much interest?"

"Fifteen cents," the banker said.

Uncle Versie popped a dime and a nickel down on that desk and he said, "Sir, give me my savings bond."

The banker smiled and said, "Mr. Ledbetter, before I give you the bond, would you please explain to me why you came into my bank and borrowed just one dollar for a year?"

"It's real simple. I needed a safe place to keep my savings bond for a year, and I talked to that lady over yonder a year ago and she explained to me that a safe deposit box cost twenty-four dollars a year. I got you to keep it for me for fifteen cents."

In my fertilizer selling days I called on some folks who started out with nothing and ended up millionaires. They probably would have done even better if they had had a good education, but they did the best they could with what they had. I remember one individual who owned a big business; we called him a "furnish merchant," because he furnished the farmers whatever they needed to get their crops started or equip their barns and houses. He bought P & G soap and flour by the carload, thousands of trace chains and well buckets. He did an enormous business, and he would carry farmers until fall, when they sold their crop. Then would come the settling up. And this man got wealthy.

The furnish merchant's son went off to Mississippi State to get a degree in accounting, came back, and took over the business as the general manager and bookkeeper. One Saturday the old gentle-

When Florence Henderson and I shared the spotlight on The Nashville Network's "Country Cooking" show, she traded her slimming fried chicken recipe for some of my totally non-fattening country humor.

man who had started the business went down to the store and saw a big sign on the front door, "Closed for inventory."

He entered through a side door and asked his boy, "What are you doing closing this store on a Saturday morning when my customers want service?"

"Papa, we got to take inventory to see how much profit we have made."

"Boy, you see that stepladder way back yonder in the corner of this store? If you'll get on that stepladder and climb up to the top you will see a piece of a bolt of cloth lying up on that top shelf. Me and your mama started this business fifty years ago with that bolt of cloth. Everything else in this store is profit. Now get that front door open!"

I'm for education. I support it, but you got to blend in a few basic elements like horse sense and motivation to make it really work.

66 **J**erry is a member of the church which I have served as pastor for nearly twenty-six years and a close, dear friend.

We are both avid sports fans. Together we have attended every Southeastern Conference Basketball Tournament since they were revived in 1979. I honestly believe Jerry knows *every* athletic director, *every* coach, and *every* sports writer in the South on a first-name basis—and they know him!

Jerry is a respected churchman. He loves the Lord and he loves his church. He has been a member of First Baptist Church in Yazoo City since 1954, a deacon most of that time, and a faithful steward of his material possessions.

Jerry loves life. He spreads joy and prompts laughter everywhere he goes.

But Jerry is serious about his relationship with Jesus Christ and seldom makes a personal appearance without mentioning this fact. He is deeply committed to family life and extols the virtues of a closely-knit Christian family. He is concerned about drug and alcohol abuse and takes advantage of every opportunity to encourage young people to live clean, moral lives.

I am proud to be Jerry Clower's pastor and personal friend. In a world filled with so much gloom and despair, it is refreshing to hear a voice of cheer and optimism. Jerry's voice echoes just that! **99**

Jerry's "Brother Jim"
James F. Yates, Pastor
First Baptist Church
Yazoo City, Mississippi

Fifteen-Yard Penalty

I was in Starkville, Mississippi, at a high school football game and right about the middle of the third quarter, the official stepped off a fifteen-yard penalty and stopped right in front of the home team's bench. The coach said, "Referee, you stink." The referee reached down and picked up that red rag and walked fifteen more yards with it before dropping it down again, turned, looked at the coach and said, "How do I smell from here?"

I enjoy being with Opry stars such as Skeeter Davis (left), a Kentuckian by birth, whose long success in the music business with greats like Eddie Arnold and Ernest Tubb led her to become a Tennessean. At right, Roy Acuff and I fellowship in his dressing room at the Opry. (Photos by Melodie Gimple)

Some of Us Aren't Gettin'
'Cause We Ain't Givin'

P robably one of the great tragedies in all of this country is that people rob themselves of the blessing of giving. I'm impressed with civic-minded people. In civic clubs across America, they do a fabulous job giving of their time and their effort, but I'm afraid there are some people in my hometown who would never miss a step if you tore down everything in this city except where they live and where they work. They don't even know we have a Chamber of Commerce. They don't even know there are civic clubs in this city to help other folks. They don't even know there is a Manor House or a mission feeding the hungry. They don't care about anything but themselves. They are robbing themselves of the great blessing of giving. That's the tragedy.

In the mid-seventies, I joined Tandy Rice and Barbara Farnsworth at an MCA Records luncheon.

We were having a discussion about giving on a call-in talk show not too long ago, and a lady asked me, "Mr. Clower, I heard somewhere you are a storehouse tither; you give ten percent of each and every dime you make to the First Baptist Church in Yazoo City, Mississippi. Then as the Lord blesses you, you give over and above your tithes."

"Yes, ma'am."

"Well, if I made the kind of money you make, I would be a storehouse tither too."

I hastened to tell the caller, "Darlin', I was a storehouse tither when I was selling fertilizer and owed everybody in Mississippi; but the Lord found me faithful when I had a little. Now he's trusting me with a bunch."

Don't rob yourself of the blessing of giving. Now some folks won't believe what I'm about to say, but if someone wrote a check for the entire budget of my church, it would not affect my giving one bit, because no one is going to take away from me the beautiful, wonderful, blessing of sharing.

I try to tithe my time like I do my money. Tandy Rice, my manager and head of Top Billing in Nashville, calls those dates "freebies." Working at Top Billing several years ago was a beautiful lady, an account executive named Barbara Farnsworth. A model, a Church of Christ Christian, and a fine representative of Top Billing, she was also a big supporter of David Lipscomb College in Nashville. At her suggestion Tandy Rice arranged a benefit for the college. Well, the late Ira North, a world-famous Church of Christ preacher, challenged the supporters of David Lipscomb College; he said, "If a Grand Ole Opry star is going to give us a night's work, the least we can do is price the tickets so we will all be making a sacrificial gift to Christian education. Tickets sold out at $500 a pair, and David Lipscomb College cleared $300,000. I had a great time performing for the people, and I left there elated because I felt the joy of giving in my heart.

Not long after that we buried the lovely Barbara Farnsworth. She had died of the same cancer that took Steve McQueen. Word went out that we were setting up a memorial to her at David Lipscomb College, and the music community got involved. They sent in about $50,000 to fund the memorial. I want to say here and now that Jerry Clower is probably the only Southern Baptist layman and Tandy Rice is probably the only Presbyterian layman in all history who have their names on a plaque in the Barbara Farnsworth Lobby at David Lipscomb College, a Church of Christ school.

The point I'm making here is simple. I was willing to give. All right, did I get from this giving? Since that show at Lipscomb, I have been booked approximately twenty times at my regular fee by Church of Christ Christian schools throughout the United States of America. I wasn't thinking about getting from performing at David Lipscomb. It was the last thing on my mind. This was a place of Christian service. I just got up and performed for the blessing of giving. By giving, I was able to get.

I hope you are not robbing yourself of giving. It is a wonderful blessing from God.

In order to be a good citizen, an individual ought to start off the first day of every week in the church of his faith worshiping God. Next, make sure you are a qualified elector and you do vote. Next, serve on the jury if you're asked to serve. And last, but not least, invest some money in local industry.

Newgene's 4-H Trip

Folks ask me about Newgene Ledbetter. Newgene was the mean one. The older he got, though, the better he got. He joined the 4-H Club and the 4-H agent taught him some sense.

I remember one year Newgene Ledbetter went off on a big 4-H Club Roundup in Chicago. Before he left he told his papa, Uncle Versie, he had to take things to swap with the other boys coming in from all over the United States.

Now at the convention some of those Yankee 4-H Club boys made fun of the Southern farm boys, but Newgene had a good time and came back with $387, all in one-dollar bills.

Uncle Versie got a dried brush broom. "Newgene, you done robbed a bank."

"I ain't done no such, Papa. I ain't done nothing wrong. I just took advantage of some ignorant people; I can't help it if they are crazy."

"Well, Newgene, how did you get this money?"

"Papa, I took a big sack of cockleburs with me, and I sold them to those Yankee boys at a dollar apiece as porcupine eggs."

✉ Straight from the U.S. Mail Bag

Dear Jerry,

Your witness across our country, both as a Christian gentleman and family man, gives testimony that show business and Christianity can "mix" and "clean" humor, enjoyed by both children and adults, is *very* successful in our society.

Sincerely,
Barbara Fly
Tennessee Baptist Convention

Are We Educated Beyond Our Intelligence?

I believe we are educated beyond our intelligence. It's been my privilege to sell fertilizer one time in my life. Some folks still think I'm in that business. I used to travel with educated folks, agronomy experts who had degrees in crops, in soils—knew how to talk equation-talk when it came to discussing different types of fertilizer.

One time I was traveling with a world famous agronomist, author of several books. We stopped for lunch at a little Delta town. I ordered fried chicken, rice, gravy, black-eyed peas, corn bread, iced tea, and banana pudding for dessert. We were about halfway through eating when I figured we needed some music. I told this Ph.D. friend, "Why don't you take a quarter over there and play some git-fiddling music?" He went over and read off all the selections but came back looking real disappointed. He said, "Jerry, I'm sorry, but there is no selection on the jukebox by any artist named "Git Fiddling." Whew—I felt sorry for that fellow.

I feel sorry for folks who take themselves too seriously, too. Don't complicate simple things. I drive a big long car and I'm thankful to the Lord I'm privileged to afford a car like that. But you know, I don't know how to work all the gadgets on that dashboard; I really don't. I was in an ice storm in Little Rock, Arkansas, last winter and had to call my fifteen-year-old daughter to find out how to get that ice off the windshield. Whoever designed that dashboard is educated beyond his intelligence!

I understand if you want to recruit an athlete for a university or college, the rule book written by the NCAA is 411 pages long. That's awful! You know almost everybody who had a hand in writing that book was a Ph.D. or most certainly a college graduate. I

The greatest test of a man's Christian faith is to be prosperous.

understand the main truth in recruiting. "You cannot give a prospective student athlete anything: board, books, or tuition, period." Well, why do you need 411 pages to say that? I guarantee you, I can take that book to any country store in the South and get some good old boys to help me rewrite it to five pages, and it'll say exactly the same thing they said in 411 pages.

I was on an airplane the other day taking off from Atlanta to Pensacola, Florida. I noticed we kept staying mighty low but I fly about two hundred days a year, and everything that's ever happened to anybody on an airplane except crashing has already happened to me.

We'd been out about thirty minutes when the captain came on the intercom. "Ladies and gentlemen," he said, "we have a problem—not a serious problem but serious enough so we've got to go back to Atlanta. We're going back to Atlanta because the way our altimeter is functioning makes it impossible for me to detect exactly what I need to know in order to fly the airplane properly." He used the word *vector*, and other fancy terms and said a lot of things about the schedule's being worked out so we would all get on down to Pensacola.

Reaching Atlanta, we dived down at the ground like we were dropping dust on boll weevils in the cotton crop. We bounced on the ground about three times and I said, "Good gracious alive. Wonder what in the world is wrong with this airplane?"

Since Fan Fair began in 1972, the popularity of this week-long enter-tainment extravaganza has grown tremendously. After arriving in style with Vernon and Tandy, I hosted the MCA Records Show. (Top two photos by Beth Gwinn)

78

As we left the plane, I stuck my head into the little cubbyhole and talked to the captain who had recognized me earlier. He asked me how Marcel Ledbetter was doing, and I said, "Captain, could you tell me in Route 4-Liberty-Mississippi-talk that Marcel Ledbetter could understand what is wrong with the airplane? Why did we have to come back to Atlanta?"

"Jerry," he said, "I didn't know how high I was, and I didn't know how fast we were going."

Well, I understood that. He finally made a statement proving he wasn't educated beyond his intelligence.

Keep it simple!

I remember when I was stationed at Oceanside, California, training with the Marines, I went to the circus with some good old boys from Alabama. A fellow came by pushing a little cart, yelling, "Hot-roasted peanuts. Get your hot-roasted peanuts." One old boy from Jackson Gap, Alabama, said, "Jerry, what in the world is that? Let's get us some of those hot-roasted peanuts. You ever heard of 'em?"

My buddy gave the fellow some money, opened the sack, reached in there and bellered, "Jerry, they ain't nothing but penders!"

We got some people in the world regardless of how educated or how simple they are, who won't *ever* admit that they have made a mistake. I answered my phone the other day—the phone that very few people know how to call me on—and I said, "Hello." This lady's voice said, "I'd like to speak to Sarah." I said, "Lady, you have the wrong number." She said, "I ain't got the wrong number; you just answered the wrong phone."

Definition of a Cow

A cow is a completely automatic milk manufacturing machine. It is encased in untanned leather and mounted on four vertical, movable supports, one on each corner. The front end contains the cutting and grinding mechanism as well as light sensors, an air inlet and exhaust, a bumper, and a foghorn.

At the rear is the dispensing apparatus and an automatic fly swatter. The central portion houses a hydro-chemical conversion plant consisting of four fermentation and storage tanks connected in series by an intricate network of flexible plumbing. This section also contains the heating plant complete with automatic temperature controls, pumping station, and main ventilating system. The waste disposal apparatus is located at the rear of the central section.

In brief, the extremely visible features are two lookers, two hookers, four stand-uppers, four hanger-downers, and a swishy wishy.

66 Jerry Clower is truly the flower of the South and a Christian to boot. What else can I say? **99**

Mel Tillis
Musician

Integration: A Mississippi Perspective

I was born in the state of Mississippi and I was educated here. I've never lived anywhere but in the state of Mississippi, and I know the state's image still suffers because of a rigid racist label pasted on it during the 1960s civil rights confrontations. It bothers me. I want to go on record insisting the rest of the country has labeled Mississippi all wrong.

Just recently Mississippi produced Mike Espy, thirty-three years old, the first black United States Representative from the state since reconstruction. My son, Ray Clower, graduated from high school with Mike Espy. Mississippi is truly an integrated state. We have more elected black public officials than any other state in the union. It didn't used to be this way, but let's give credit where credit is due.

The way things were used to really bother me when I was a boy. Back then, blacks traveling through the state didn't have a place to eat, sleep, or go to the bathroom. At the time that was true in a lot of states. I fought a war to give an individual the right to be a bigot if he wanted to be. That happens to be a constitutional right. But it is not a constitutional right for bigots to make up a majority of the lawmaking bodies. That was our problem back then. Bigots controlled the legislature, and we had laws to discriminate against black people. Now, anyone can travel comfortably through the state of Mississippi. Now bigots are not in control. The law says you cannot mistreat anybody, and Mississippi complies.

Not long ago, at the Atlanta airport, I was playing with a little boy in the waiting room near one of the concourses. It was crowded and the little boy ran so hard he tripped, fell, and butted the bottom of one of those chairs bolted to the floor knocking a pretty good gash in his head. Blood was spurting from the cut and his mother

Mississippi State's football coach, Emory Bellard, cashed in on a good publicity bet by establishing a country connection when I met—not country singers, but MSU gridiron men—Johnny Cash (left), and Kenny Rogers (right).

was upset. Right away an airline employee called for medics, but before they arrived, an immaculately dressed, good-looking black gentleman eased up to me and said quietly, "Mr. Clower, I am a medical doctor. Would you ask the mother if it would be all right for me to check the little boy?"

Well, my heart got heavy, I knew where he was coming from. He was afraid to just go to the boy's mother and say, "I'm a doctor. Let me check your little boy." Had he been white, he would have.

I told the mother of his offer and immediately she asked for the doctor's help. The doctor opened up a little satchel, got a pressure bandage, and fixed the cut, urging her to seek the advice of a plastic surgeon when they reached home. About that time the medics arrived with all their equipment and checked the little boy, but they said everything had been done already.

I hope one day we grow to the point where an individual can perform as a professional, whatever his race, nationality, or origin.

Leontyne Price is one of the greatest Mississippians. Mississippi raised her and, let me hasten to say, she has raised the state of Mississippi. After a concert in Jackson, Mississippi, one night, Miss Price received several standing ovations. Almost tearfully she told her audience, "I cannot tell you how wonderful it is to come home."

Well said, Leontyne Price. You were talking about my home state, too.

We have made changes in the state of Mississippi that are wholesome and right, and the rights of others are exhibited in this state as well as any state in the union. If we fail sometimes, it's because someone has forgotten making "rights" work requires each one of us to be responsible for the way we treat other folks. Each one of us can make a difference in creating a better place to live.

✉ Straight from the U.S. Mail Bag

Dear Jerry:

I offer you my congratulations for being honored by your hometown folks. You have certainly come a long way since I knew you as a fertilizer salesman from Yazoo City. When I was assistant coach at Mississippi State, I knew you had potential. I sat right behind you at a few basketball games and you had the "loudest booming" voice I have ever heard!

You are a great service to your fellowmen by helping them laugh and have fun. The greatest honor that can come to anyone is to be appreciated and honored by those closest to you.

You have reached the apex! If you don't know what apex means, I will get Jim Champion or Dave "Dog" Owens to explain it to you sometime.

Sincerely,
John Majors
Head Football Coach
Assistant Director of Athletics
University of Tennessee

Counterfeiters

B ack when I was a young'un growing up, a big counterfeit ring was working out of St. Louis, Missouri. One of its engraving machines went haywire and printed a bunch of fifteen-dollar bills.

The counterfeiters got around their table and said, "What are we going to do with these fifteen-dollar bills?"

"I'll tell you what we will do. We'll go down to Mississippi where they are kind of dumb, go to one of those country stores, and get the bills changed for good money."

They were riding down through Highway 24, Route 4, Liberty, Mississippi, when they saw Mr. Duvall Scott's store and stopped. Duvall's shoes were overrun and one gallus was off his overalls. He didn't look too sharp. They said, "Sir, do you run this store?"

"I do."

"Well, I got a fifteen-dollar bill here I would like to get changed."

"Beautiful. I'll be glad to do it for you."

He rang the cash register and said, "How would you like it? You want two sixes and a three, or would you rather have five three dollar bills?"

To be successful, be courteous, hustle, and be yourself.

We Need Broad-Bottomed Architects

I grew up in a shotgun house, vowing one day to live in a house that wasn't so small.

A shotgun house is the cheapest form of construction known to man. It's just a straight house. You could shoot a shotgun through the front door and the shot would travel all the way through the house and come out the back door. That's a shotgun house.

Skimpy spaces bother me. I would like to see a new association formed, the National Association for Broad-Bottomed Architects, professionals who would always keep sufficient space in mind—breathing room.

When I get on an airplane and have to suck up and force myself down in the seat, put my knees under my chin and fly for about an hour-and-a-half, I say the architect who designed that cotton-picking seat had to be about twelve-inches broad across the rump, and I get aggravated.

I get more aggravated when I check into a motel or a hotel and see those little bitty chairs. It's obvious people who own some motels and some hotels never spend the night in their own facility, because if they did, they'd make things bigger. Especially bathrooms. We need broad-bottomed architects to design bathrooms. Take the showers. Someone has decided that the old-fashioned, two-faucet system isn't sufficient. Now folks, nothing could be simpler than to reach over on the left and turn on the hot water faucet. Then when it gets hot, reach over on the right, turn on the cold water and homogenize the cold and hot until they blend into the warmth you want. Then you pull that little knob and let the shower come down on you. That's real simple. Now someone has combined those faucets into one knob and sometimes I feel like taking an engineer on the road with me to show me how to figure out the whole business! The worst are the long prongs that stick out into the shower area. You catch hold of one and try to suggest to it what water temperature you like. Then when you get the water flowing just right, you discover this architect is about nine inches across the bottom because he has moved the curtain rod over to where it's directly above the inside of the bathtub, and the shower curtain is hanging straight down from it. Now if he would move the curtain rod over to the outside of the bathtub, not only would it be out of your way and not come down on your shoulder, but the water would be slanted running down on this curtain and it would even function better. But you finally get that one-knobbed faucet straightened out and the water is pouring down on your body and the draft has got that little flimsy shower curtain flopping all up on your leg and up between your legs, and you reach around with the soap to try to lather over yonder and your leg bumps that big old long snout coming out from the faucet. Ohhhhhhhh! It's hog-scalding time! You have bumped into that prong, nudged it out of position, scalded yourself, and you have to start all over again. What this country needs is broad-bottomed architects who will design facilities big enough for men—not boys.

I don't guess I can blame architects for the size of some of these cars, but somebody has figured out that everybody in America wants a small car—not me. I try not to ride in a car that I look better walking or toting than riding in.

If a man is genuinely converted, if he becomes a child of God, then he couldn't break into hell if he tried. That's just the way it works.

✉ Straight from the U.S. Mail Bag

Dear Tandy:

I recently had the privilege of producing *Ain't God Good!*, a film on the life and work of Jerry Clower. I have never had a more enjoyable working experience.

Jerry Clower loves life and he loves people. This is clearly shown in his commitment to the Lord, as well as his commitment to his family and fellow human beings. He is a breath of fresh air to our world, and I am very proud to have worked with Mr. Clower and consider him a friend.

This film featured Mr. Clower sharing some of his best stories and personal testimony. After releasing the film to churches and Christian groups around the country, I showed it to The Nashville Network. They wanted me to recut the film into a half-hour comedy special. This means the stories Jerry tells in church, he also features in live performances at county fairs, television stations, civic clubs, etc., everywhere. Jerry Clower is the same man before a church audience as before a secular audience.

Most people cannot even begin to fathom the generosity and love of Jerry Clower. First of all, when I produced the film *Ain't God Good!* for churches, Mr. Clower received absolutely no financial compensation for this show whatsoever. And when I approached him and his agent, Tandy Rice, about recutting *Ain't God Good!* into a special for The Nashville Network, which we later entitled *The Mouth of the South*, they simply told me that whatever funds I could make from The Nashville Network, I should apply to the budget of my Christian film. Again, they received no compensation for this project. I am also well aware that not only does Mr. Clower tithe his income on a yearly basis, but he also tithes his time by speaking in scores of churches, to youth groups, and in prisons throughout the country. Mr. Clower is a wonderful, giving man, and I wish more people knew of all he does for his fellow human beings.

Charles Warren
Life Productions

87

A Box for Clovis

We used to refer to Clovis Ledbetter as someone whose "bread wasn't quite done."

When I was visiting Marcel the other day, Clovis came up to me and said, "You reckon that lumber company you do commercials for would make me a box 2½"x 2½"x 51' long?"

I said, "Clovis, are you crazy? No! They can make you a box, but why in the world would you want a box 2½"x 2½"x 51' long?"

He said, "My neighbor, the farmer over yonder, is a sharecropper and he just moved off and left his garden hose. I wanna mail it to him."

Jeannie C. Riley was one of many friends who visited Yazoo City for the opening of Jerry Clower Boulevard.

The Local Church Is Where It's At

A dictionary defines *church* as a building for public Christian worship. I feel the first place of Christian service for any Christian is through the local church. I'm asked just about every day of my life to give to something or to participate in something good. I believe in most of the things I'm asked to participate in by giving money or time, but I never, ever, get involved in anything in direct competition with the local church. And I truly believe the first place of Christian service for any Christian ought to be in the local church.

I've seen some real humorous things in my life at church. I remember during a revival meeting, a very fine lady was sitting in the Amen corner with her grandson. He was squirming and talking continually so this dear old lady leaned over and whispered to him in her deep voice, "Behave!" Now her voice in a whisper carried all over the church and jarred the pews it was so loud. About three times she leaned over that little boy, and put her lips right up to his ear, and whispered, "Boy, if you don't be quiet, I'm goin' to kill ya." You could hear it plain as day. "Boy, if you don't be quiet, I'm goin' to kill ya." Well, the little fellow kept disturbing the worship so this old lady gathered him up and started down the aisle toward the back door and just as she went out the little boy waved and yelled, "Bye, bye, everybody."

The local church is where it's at, folks.

Many of our churches today have facilities and programs to fit everybody. A dear friend in Nashville wanted to talk to me the other day; he knows I'm happily married and enjoy a happy home where love is. I asked him, "What is your burden?"

"Jerry, I'm in love with a woman who doesn't love me."

"Cull her and let me give you some advice. You go to one of

these big churches in Nashville; there's one right across from the Opry House with a wonderful singles department. Get active in the singles department of that local church, and you can pick you out a young lady who will love you. In fact, you can find one kind of plump inasmuch as you are overweight. You can even walk through one of their social functions and smell the kind of perfume you like. You'll probably find some young lady with the same burden as yours. You can become acquainted and start a courtship in the local church. I recommend that to you. I recommend that to anybody."

A lot of people say, "We just don't have facilities to compete with the world. Our children are so tempted." Well, let me tell you, my daughter Sue once refused a trip to Hollywood that I had been describing in glowing terms because she didn't want to miss something scheduled at the church activities building. After she refused, I picked up the phone and called the youth director of my church, and I said, "Sir, do you need anything?"

The local church can compete with the world and I'm so proud that on Friday evening my children have regularly come through the den saying, "We are going to the building." They won't get hooked on anything down at the church except developing a habit that's good and wholesome for them.

My first place of Christian service is through the local church. The local church needs to be supported with our attendance, with our tithes and offerings, and with our prayers, because the local church is where it's at.

At a performance in Raleigh, North Carolina's Reynolds Coliseum, I met David Byrd, son of Martha and Billy Byrd. He walked right into my arms there and later visited me in Yazoo City.

✉ Straight from the U.S. Mail Bag

Mr. Tandy Rice
Top Billing, Inc.
P.O. Box 121089
Nashville, TN

Dear Mr. Rice:

I would just like to take a moment to compliment one of the stars you represent, Mr. Jerry Clower.

. . . Jerry is such a warm and interested human being that he took the time [while in North Carolina] to make a young blind boy feel important. His outpouring of love to this young boy is truly an inspiration. I wanted to tell you how proud we are to have Jerry performing at the North Carolina State Fair. We know he will be a good drawing card.

Jerry is a great American and a real friend of agriculture and all people.

Sincerely,
James A. Graham
Commissioner of Agriculture
North Carolina

Three Wise Men

We were in Sunday School one morning back in days gone by. Me and Marcel Ledbetter never missed a Sunday. The teacher was quizzing us. She asked Marcel, "What was the occupation of the three wise men?"

"They were fahrmen."

"Why in the world would you think they were firemen?"

" 'Cause the Bible plainly says, 'They come from afahr.' "

Homerline's Hollerin' Goody

2 tablespoons flour
1/2 cup sugar
3 eggs
1/4 cup soft butter
Pinch salt
1 cup Karo light syrup
1 cup pecan pieces ·
1 unbaked 9-inch pie shell

Mix flour with sugar. Beat eggs slightly and add softened butter, a pinch of salt, the sugar mixture, Karo and pecan pieces. Pour into pie shell. (I pick some up at the store). Bake in a preheated oven at 350 degrees for 50 minutes.

Suggestions from Homerline: Serve with a pot of fresh, hot coffee. Plan to bake more than one of these at a time, because the first one goes so fast the folks who didn't get any will be hollerin' for a piece.

Negativism: Shake It Off!

Everywhere I go I meet negative people—and I'm trying to stamp out negativism.

I'm interviewed everywhere I go, and I don't mind it. I believe people who cuss the press have something to hide. The press has been good to me. Every time a piece appears about me, I sell a few more records. I'm human enough to like that.

Every now and then, though, some interviewer will ask me a question that if answered truthfully makes me sound negative. I was doing the Grand Ole Opry not too long ago on The Nashville Network, and after my routine I started off stage. There stood an NBC news/radio personality. I could tell he wanted to do something negative, because he looked like he just got over a hookworm treatment.

Mel Tillis and I laugh on the job, in this case a Purina commercial—a memorable event for both of us since the director had ordered, "No stammering allowed!"

The Hank Snow Child Abuse Foundation hosted a spectacular benefit show at the Opry House in 1983. I was one of Hank Snow's guests (top left) along with (clockwise) Mickey Gilley, T. Tommy Cutrer, and Ricky Skaggs.

"Mr. Clower," he said, "a lot of you Grand Ole Opry stars are booked in Europe, but I'm sure in the next few months, you'll cancel your European trip on account of terrorism and the danger of Kadafi." And then he stuck that microphone up in my face for my reply.

"Sir, I'm what's known as a good ole boy. I grew up in the South, and a lot of us good ole boys aren't scared of Kadafi. Not only is Kadafi a world-famous terrorist, but he's also a world-famous liar. He's got people in this country thinking it's more dangerous to fly to Europe than it is to drive through Atlanta. Statistics show that one out of fourteen hundred Americans who travels in this country will be injured, and one out of seven hundred thousand who travels to Europe will be injured. If Delta Airlines will let its captains and flight attendants fly to Europe, I will fly to Europe whenever I dad-blamed please."

The dear man was stunned. I was supposed to whine and cry about how dangerous it is to fly to Europe. Then he looked at me and said, "Well, Mr. Clower, what if Kadafi and the terrorists blow up your airplane?"

"Sir, I've got a home in heaven."

"Well, what if Kadafi and the terrorists kidnap you?"

"I'll get Jesse Jackson to come and get me."

I wish everybody could have the attitude of a certain twelve-year-old in Yazoo City, Mississippi. He wanted to play baseball the other day but didn't have anybody to play with him. That boy kept pestering his mother to play with him but she said, "Son, I'm busy. Just get out in the yard and play by yourself." He went out in the backyard with his baseball and bat, threw the ball up in the air, drew back his bat, swung at it and missed. He threw the ball up a second time, drew back, took careful aim, swung at it, and missed again. He threw the ball up for a third time, drew back, swung at it, and missed a third time. And that spunky fellow threw his head back, smiled, and hollered, "Gosh, what a pitcher!"

It's hard to misunderstand love. If you convince folks you are interested in them because you love them, then you've just about got them—it's hard to fight love.

We have a negative barber in our town. I've been praying for him for thirty years. You go in his barber shop and the sun may be shining bright. But if you say, "It's a pretty day today, isn't it?" he'll say, "It'll be raining in an hour." If I weren't a Christian I'd hire somebody to kill him.

My buddy Bill went into the barber shop and that old pessimistic barber said, "Bill, I hear you're going to take a trip."

"Yeah, I'm going to catch TWA airlines to Rome, and I'm gonna visit with the Pope."

That old pessimistic barber groaned, "TWA is the sorriest airline in the world. They'll lose your suitcase. They ain't never on time. If you make it to Rome on that sorry airline, Rome will stink this time of the year. You ain't gonna get to see that Pope. I guarantee you, you ain't gonna get to see that Pope. If you see that Pope, you'll stand out there with a hundred thousand people hoping that he walks out on that there porch up yonder on the side of the wall."

Old Bill was back in the barber shop about a month later and that pessimistic barber said, "Bill, you didn't take that stupid trip did you?"

"I did take that trip and you lied to me. TWA is a good airline. They didn't lose my suitcase. The flight attendants were friendly, and we landed in Rome right on time. I took a whiff of Rome, and you lied about that; Rome wasn't stinking. You were right about one thing. There were a hundred thousand people all scrunched up together hoping the Pope would walk out on that little old shelf up yonder on the side of the wall."

And that old pessimistic barber said, "You didn't get to see him either, did you, Bill?"

"I most certainly did see him. While I was standing there hoping that the Pope would walk out on that shelf, a fellow pulled at my sleeve and said, 'Hey, buddy, come with me; the Pope sent me after you.'

"We got on an elevator, and went up three floors; the elevator door opened, and there stood the Pope. We were one-on-one, eyeball-to-eyeball. I stuck out my hand and I said, 'Brother Pope, my it's good to see you. This is the highlight of my trip getting to see you one-on-one.'"

That old pessimistic barber said, "Bill, why did the Pope pick

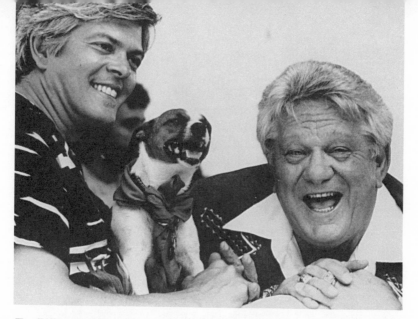

Top Billing President Tandy Rice, his dog, Vernon, and I enjoy each other's company. Vernon, a female of great charm, accompanies Tandy to his Music City office every day. (Photo by Beth Gwinn)

you out of all them people and bring you up there as an individual and visit with you?''

Bill said, "I wondered the same thing so I asked him, 'Why did you pick me out of all those folks and bring me up here?'

'Young man,' the Pope said, 'I wanted to pray with you and counsel with you because out of a hundred thousand people, you undoubtedly had the sorriest haircut of anybody I ever saw.'''

One of the most negative people I have ever known in my life was Clovis Ledbetter. Clovis was so negative he didn't even want to be a Ledbetter; he always wanted to be a log truck. When Clovis was a little boy, you'd call, "Clovis, Clovis." He'd say, "Rummmm, rummmm, rummm." If Clovis got stuck in a mud hole during recess at school, you'd hear his engine straining, "Ying, ying, ying, ying." If you were standing behind him, he'd kick mud all over you. If you moved around in front of him, he would put himself in reverse and "ying, ying, ying" kick it forward. Well, one day Clovis was in the back of the classroom idling. Miss Minnie Lee Stone, the teacher, yelled, "Clovis, shut up that racket." Clovis just mouthed, "IRRRRRRRRR" and slammed on the brakes.

Clovis Ledbetter made noises like a log truck until he was twenty-two years old. You know what got Clovis to talking? Girls. Azlee DeLaughter, the ugliest female God ever allowed to be birthed in all Mississippi, flung a craving on Clovis. Azlee had to slip up on the dipper to get a drink of water. If Moses had seen Azlee we would have had another commandment. But old Clovis wooed Azlee, courted her, married her, and built him a little house out there on Uncle Versie Ledbetter's farm.

One Monday morning old Clovis was digging postholes because it was the right time of the moon to dig a posthole. (Am I confusing you—"the right time of the moon to dig a posthole?" I hope you are as cultured as I am; if you're not, I love you anyway. I thought everybody knew if you dig a posthole the wrong time of the moon, there won't be enough a dirt to go back in the hole.)

A brand new preacher had just moved into the county and didn't know a soul. He'd been walking those dirt roads, visiting folks, for three weeks. He was trying to motivate folks to come to church the next Lord's Day, and he walked up to Clovis and said, "Sir, are you a Christian?"

Clovis said, "No, I'm a Ledbetter."

"Sir, you don't understand. Are you lost?"

Clovis said, "Heck, no, I ain't lost, I was born in that house right yonder."

"You still don't understand," the preacher insisted. "Are you ready for resurrection day?"

"When's that gonna be?"

"Well, nobody knows. It could be today; it could be tomorrow."

Clovis said, "Don't you tell my wife; she'll wanna' go both days."

Uncle Versie Ledbetter had a mule named Della. One day Della fell in a cistern Uncle Versie thought he had covered up, but hadn't. Old Della stumbled and fell down in that thing about thirty feet. The cistern hadn't been used in a long, long time because the REA had run in electricity and with a pump Uncle Versie had no need for a cistern to be catching rainwater.

Well, Uncle Versie had a problem. There was his best mule down at the bottom of that cistern and no way he could get the mule out of there. He didn't want her to stay down there and starve to death, and so he decided he would get a shovel and cover her up. It would be cruel but it wouldn't be as cruel and inhumane as to let Della starve to death in the bottom of that deep cistern. Uncle Versie took a shovelful of dirt and threw it down into the cistern and every time a shovelful of dirt would hit old Della, she'd shake the dirt off and stomp it. He kept throwing dirt down and Della kept shaking that dirt off and stomping it. It wasn't long before Della had shaken off enough dirt and stomped it so she was high enough to jump out of the cistern.

Are you negative? Are you spreading negativism? Please shake it off; shake it off!

You prove your love for your children if you make them behave more than if you let them misbehave. Letting them misbehave just isn't fair to the child.

Running the Coon

The smartest dog in all the world was a dog named Highball that belonged to Uncle Versie Ledbetter. Folks used to come from all over the country just to see old Highball run. Beautiful dog with a beautiful voice. One time a city fellow came all the way from Jackson, Mississippi, to *hear* old Highball run.

Highball jumped a rabbit. He was right in behind it . . . running and barking, and barking and running, and the man from Jackson said, "Oh, ain't that beautiful. Listen, listen." About that time Highball quit barking. Then three minutes later he started back up again—just barking away. The man said, "What happened there? Why did he stop barking all of a sudden and now he's at it again?" Uncle Versie said, "Well, Highball was running across *posted* land."

Duane Allen of the Oak Ridge Boys and I share a smile at Fan Fair. (Photo by Beth Gwinn)

Working Hands Get Respect

Ask a construction worker about some individual on the job, that man will say "He is a *hand*," meaning that person is a good worker. Americans still admire hard workers, and I'm so pleased about that. If you aren't lazy, you are respected. Folks just don't like lazy people. Have you ever picked up a hitchhiker? I'm sure at sometime in your life you probably have. How many times have you ever picked up a hitchhiker sitting or lying down beside the road? Not only do I not pick them up, I scatter 'em. My wife and I were driving out of Jackson, Mississippi, the other day going north. We rounded a big old curve and saw two hitchhikers: one lying down with his head on his suitcase, the other sitting with his back against an old knapsack. They both had their fists stuck up and their thumbs shining, and I felt my wife's hand come over on my leg. She said, "No, Jerry, no, they're not hurtin' you." Well, I was tempted to send them down that bank. If they want to ride with me they need to stand up on their tiptoes ready to chase my car if I slow down to pick them up. People respect folks who aren't lazy.

Marcel Ledbetter was my dearest friend when I was growing up because he wasn't lazy. He was a working hand. He really, really could do it. In fact, when we were cutting stove wood, he wouldn't ride the crosscut saw. (When you pull your end of the crosscut toward you, sometimes the partner on the other end of the log will mash down on the saw to make you do most of the cutting. But not Marcel. Marcel would hang in there and pull his side of the load.)

Marcel Ledbetter is still a working hand. He's a retired navy man with a good living, but he still doesn't want just to loaf all the time, so he drives an automobile transport rig part time hauling new cars all over this country.

Marcel was in his rig the other day between Clarksdale, Mississippi, and Tunika, on the longest, straightest, flattest stretch of

Big Mama's Blueberry Pie

1 cup sugar
1 stick margarine, melted
2 eggs
2 tablespoons flour
1 cup berries (Wild huckleberries may be used.)
1 unbaked 9-inch pie crust

Mix sugar, margarine, eggs and flour. Put berries in uncooked pie crust and pour sugar mixture over berries. Bake at 350 degrees 30 to 35 minutes.

road in the world. He was just burning up that highway about midnight, whistling and having a good time when the lights went out on that rig.

Marcel couldn't continue in the dark, but he noticed one of those new cars was resting right up above the cab of his truck with the lights pointing down toward the ground. So Marcel had an idea. He climbed up on top of the cab of his rig, opened the door of that new car, turned on its lights and studied how they shone right down on the road. He shut the door on that new car, got back in his rig, cranked it up and was doing pretty good driving along, using the new car's lights from way up above the cab of his rig. It wasn't long before he met a car. And this car, when it got about a hundred yards from Marcel's transport rig, veered off the road and took to the cotton patch, knocking cotton bolls and cotton everywhere. Marcel finally got his rig stopped, ran out through the cotton patch, opened the door of the car and said, "Mister, are you hurt?"

The man driving the car said, "No, I'm not hurt."

"Well, what in the world is wrong? Why did you go off the road?"

"Mister, I figured if you were as wide as you were tall I'd better give you the whole highway."

❖ ❖ ❖

Sometimes I get down on one knee to communicate with the Opry audience.
(Photo by Melodie Gimple)

Marcel doesn't have a lazy bone in his body. He is so against being lazy that he milks his own cow. Now Marcel doesn't sell any milk; he just has his own personal milk cow in a little shed right out on the edge of the lot. One evening kind of late he was out there milking that cow. He had put the bucket down and set himself on the milk stool, his head leaning over the cow's flank, and he was two handed—swish, swish, swish, swish. He had foamed up that bucket. A city fellow pulled up in the yard, got out of the car, walked out there, stuck his head through the shed door and said, "Mister, can you tell me how to get to Bogue Chitto, Mississippi?"

"You're heading in the right direction. Just keep going straight toward McComb, and you'll hit the interstate about ten miles from here. Head north on the interstate, and you won't go very far 'til you see an exit marked Bogue Chitto."

"Thank you," the man said. He turned around and started back toward his car. Marcel started milking again but in a little bit the fellow reappeared at the door.

"Sir, can you tell me what time it is?"

Marcel said, "Yeah, let me see." He opened up his hands real wide, put them up under the udder of that milk cow. He let those spouts hang down between his fingers and he shoved with even pressure, both hands up on the bag of that cow. He raised up the bag, and brought his head down, looked around at the man and said, "It's 5:30."

"Mister, can you country folks feel up under the cow's udder and tell what time it is?"

Marcel said, "Yeah, you want me to show you?"

"I surely do."

Marcel said, "Sit down here on this milk stool, spread your hands out like I did, put both of them up under that udder, let them sookums go down between your fingers and with even pressure bring the cow's bag up and your head down. Now, you ought to be able to see that clock on the wall right over there."

✉ Straight from the U.S. Mail Bag

Dear Mr. Clower,

If I could have one wish in this world it would be to have one neighbor on each side and both of them be Jerry Clower.

Nelda

Editor's Note: This epistle, on lined notebook paper, was handed to Jerry at one of his recent appearances.

Mr. Duvall Scott's Chicken

A visit to Mr. Duvall Scott's old store in Liberty, Mississippi, brought back a lot of fond memories. Right after the Depression when ice trucks first started running out in the county, you could buy a block of ice if you had you a few pennies. Well, Mr. Duvall Scott made a wooden icebox and started selling frying-size chickens. I have carried many a frying-size chicken to Mr. Duvall Scott and swapped that chicken for a jar of anti-pain oil or a bottle of vanilla extract. Mr. Duvall Scott would then pick the chicken, dress it, and put it in the icebox with the little chipped-up ice.

One day I was sitting in the store and a lady walked in. "I would like to buy a chicken," she said.

Duvall didn't have but one in that whole refrigerator icebox, so he reached down in there, swished it around in the water with those few little blocks of ice, brought it out and slung the water off it, put it on the scales, and said, "It weighs two-and-a-half pounds."

She said, "I want one just a little bit bigger than that."

He took that one chicken, rammed it back down in there and started stirring the ice again, stirring it good, brought up the chicken again, put it on the scales: "Three pounds."

"Fine," she said. "I'll take both of them."

Joggers, Clabber, Fiber, and Bran

I have to do a lot of praying to keep from hating all flat-bellied joggers . . . joggers who eat yogurt and don't know it's clabber. When I was growing up we had one old milk cow, and sometimes the calf would break through the fence and suck her dry. You would go in the house hunting a glass of milk and the only thing you found was a crock of clabber. Thick blue whey—slick, sour clabber. We used to get a cup, scoop it up, put it in a tall glass, get a long-handled spoon, and go to jobbing it to bust up the lumps. Sometimes we put molasses in to yellow it up and sweeten it and then we'd whirl it around and drink it. We drank it because that's all we had.

After doing a show in New York City, I was trying to unwind and get drowsy in my room at the Park Lane Hotel. A Frenchman appeared on the TV set droning away, "Yoplait yogurt," he said, "Yoplait yogurt with fruit." And I jumped up and yelled at the TV, "Clabber and huckleberries, clabber and huckleberries." Just think, when I was a boy in the depth of the Depression fifty years ago, if I had picked a handful of huckleberries and thrown them into a crock of clabber, we would have had the very latest fancy uptown yogurt with fruit.

If you are a jogger and you know in your heart you are helping your health, I respect you—more power to you. But a lot of my friends are hurting themselves because they saw somebody on a talk show recommend jogging. That fellow on the talk show is selling tennis shoes. That's what he's doing. The man who wrote the book on jogging died in the act, so make sure if you're jogging you know it's something that will be good for you.

Sometimes the best information you get is not accurate. Let

Ben Smathers (left), leader of the Stoney Mountain Cloggers, my personal manager Tandy Rice, and I exchange stories. The Stoney Mountain Cloggers have been Opry members since 1957.

me give you an illustration. In 1969, I was selling fertilizer in the citrus-growing area of Florida. I pulled a muscle in my side. Whew, it hurt! After flying to Jackson, Mississippi, by way of Tampa and Atlanta, I finally made it to King's Daughters Hospital in Yazoo City, Mississippi. Nurses there got on the intercom and paged my doctor who came to the emergency room and stuck a thermometer in my mouth.

"Doc, I pulled a muscle in my side."

"Big man, that's a hot spot right there. You got a high temperature, and I do believe you have diverticulitis. I'll give you a series of simple tests and then we'll know whether you have diverticulitis or not."

Folks, I love everybody. Let me prove to you that I love you. I want to warn you about something. If you go to the hospital for any reason, and you remotely think you hear the word *Procto*, don't let 'em get you. Gather your split-tail gown around you, and go hide in the nearest swamp. Don't let them get you. After that test I added a clause to my will: If my wife ever allows anybody to do that to me again, she'll never spend a dime of my money. Not one penny!

They strapped me to a sawhorse, turned me bottom-side up,

107

unbreached a 410-gauge shotgun (they did take the sight off the barrel), and when the sweat was popping off my forehead, I tried to look around at my doctor, like a mule peeping around a new blind bridle.

"Doctor, I don't know what it is you're doing, but when you get done, anything that I'll ever have had wrong with me, you cured it right now."

I did have diverticulitis, and my doctor told me, "Jerry, eat one more tablespoon full of bran, one more tablespoonful of fiber, and your diverticuli will get infected. You once again will have diverticulitis, and your belly may swell up like a cow bloated on white clover. You could be walking down the street and just blow up and drown a bunch of people. Whatever you do, do not eat fiber or bran.

For ten years I didn't eat anything fit to eat. Nothing. One day back in the doctor's office with one of my daughters, the doctor said, "Jerry, I have a bulletin from the American Medical Association saying right here that scientific research has now proven that fiber and bran will cure diverticulitis."

I don't blame my doctor for anything. He was using the best medical advice he could get at the time, but folks, if you're jogging, make sure it's helping you.

Airport Goodbyes

One day Marcel Ledbetter sent word he wanted to take a trip with me. We met on a Sunday morning at the Jackson, Mississippi, airport and he said, "Jerry, I'm going to fly to Boston with you."

I said, "All right, Marcel, I'll be glad to have you."

We were checking in at Delta Airlines where we noticed four people standing over in the corner squalling and crying. A fellow was hugging an older man and woman and telling them goodbye. That saddened me because I have had a few goodbyes in my time, and I don't think they're much fun. Then the man put his arm around a younger woman and approached the entrance to the snout that goes up into the airplane. He held this young woman, and they looked lovingly at one another and squalled. Finally, he put his head down and disappeared up the runway. Then the older couple and young woman commenced to squalling. By then Marcel and I were wailing. About that time the man stuck his head around the opening of the passageway and waved at the three people. "See y'all Tuesday," he said.

✉ Straight from the U.S. Mail Bag

DELTA 1657/13 BNA-ATL IS HIS FLIGHT
FOR HE IS QUITE A SIGHT
HUMOR IS HIS THEME
EVEN THOUGH THE BULLDOGS ARE HIS TEAM
ARRIVING FRESH AS A MORNING FLOWER
GET READY, ATLANTA, HERE COMES JERRY CLOWER

Editor's Note: Message sent from Delta Counter, Nashville, to Delta Counter in Atlanta.

Clower Good'uns

I'm back in Nashville minding my own business a while ago and one of my dear friends backstage at the Opry walks up to me and says, "Jerry, I see you got the furniture disease."

I said, "What?"

He said, "The furniture disease. Your chest has done dropped down into your drawers."

When I was a young'un growing up, the main-most sport was marbles. Whatever happened to playing marbles? We would draw a great big circle in the dirt, put the marbles in the center of the circle, get down on one knee and we would come to the taw. We would shoot that good aggie, the taw we called it, at the marbles, and however many you knocked out were yours. You could keep them . . . if your mama did not find out.

I remember one time my brother, Sonny, played hooky from school. He liked to help work on the old bulldozers the men were using to build a highway. One day they were working on a bulldozer and they found some steel aggie ball bearings. Well, Sonny never had seen any of them. Man, he decided he would come to school with five of them. He gave me three. When my buddies piled all their marbles in the circle, and I got down there with that steel aggie, man, I busted up the game!

We had a fellow named Ben DeLaughter. He was meaner in school than Marcel Ledbetter was. He was forevermore vicious. (He had been in the eighth grade eight times.) I was scared of him as I was of a bear. Ben said, "I want you to give me one of them steel marbles."

"I can't do it, Ben."

He commenced whipping on me 'til the bell rung and we ran in the schoolhouse. Ben sat in that little old desk and whispered, "I'm gonna beat you to death if you don't give me one of them big steel marbles."

I didn't know how in the world I was going to get away from Ben, but I eased out of my desk and went back to the stove in back

110

of the study hall like I was cold. I took two of those big aggies, those steel marbles, and put them on top of the stove. I got them scalding hot. Then I picked them up wearing a brand new pair of Red Ryder gloves I had gotten for Christmas, the ones with fringe on the side and Red Ryder's picture up on the top; Santa Claus had brought them to me.

I put those red-hot aggies down on that little trench for a pencil on the top of my desk, right there by the hole where your ink bottle was supposed to go. Then when I laid those two hot aggies up there, I went to the pencil sharpener like I was going to sharpen my pencil.

Miss Minnie Lee Stone, the teacher, had us studying; she was just sitting up there at her desk. Big Ben saw those aggies on my desk. He came easing up there like he wasn't up to anything so the teacher would not get on him. He had on a right brand new pair of overalls; he squatted down and that back pocket was open right there, and he took his pencil and raked those aggies in his back pocket—just like nothing had happened. He eased back to his desk

Big Mama's Tea Cakes

1 cup butter
1 heaping cup granulated sugar
2 eggs
$1/2$ teaspoon salt
1 teaspoon baking soda
3 cups flour
3 tablespoons buttermilk
1 teaspoon vanilla
Dash granulated sugar

Cream butter and sugar; add eggs. Add dry ingredients alternately to buttermilk/vanilla mixture. Spoon tablespoon-sized drops of batter on slightly greased cookie sheet and sprinkle with a dash of granulated sugar. Bake at 350 degrees for 8 to 13 minutes depending on how large the cakes are.

Not a bird, not a plane, it's a Clower in a Cypress Gardens, Florida, phone booth promoting "Nashville on the Road," a syndicated television show Jim Ed Brown and I co-hosted for six years.

and sat down right quick. Wowwwwwww! He started jumping up and down in that desk and he was hung in it, overgrown as he was.

Miss Minnie Lee Stone ran toward him with the paddle and commenced to beating him. "Hush! Ben, what are you screaming about, boy? You got ants in your pants?"

"No, ma'am," he said. "Hot steel balls!"

Uncle Versie Ledbetter was a great fellow. I remember one day the WMU of the Baptist church was meeting with Aunt Pet, and Uncle Versie was out in the garden sticking beans. Come time to serve refreshments, Aunt Pet called Uncle Versie.

"Versie, come on in, hon, you want to eat a piece of pie with the women?"

Uncle Versie said, "I believe I will."

They all sat around the table, and Aunt Pet had wiped the new oilcloth off real good.

Uncle Versie came in and sat down. Aunt Pet was trying a new recipe—hot apple pie. She had always left her apple pies out on the windowsill and got them cool—but these were hot! Uncle Versie didn't know this, and all the WMU women were sitting around the table, fanciest women in East Fork community. Uncle Versie forked up a great big fine swath of that pie and threw it up in his mouth and wallowed it around where it commenced to take all the hide off his tongue! Whooo!!

Uncle Versie drew back and ejected that pie, "Phoot! Sph!" Then he wiped his mouth and said, "You know, many a fool would have tried to swallow that!"

I went to see Marcel Ledbetter the other day; his brother Claud was the only one in the community catching any fish. Old Claud Ledbetter would come in from the river with a pickup truck loaded down. Well, a game warden from the State Game and Fish Commission of Mississippi decided he would go fishing with Claud just to see how he was doing it. Claud had told everyone, "Hot dog, y'all don't know how to do it. Y'all ought to just go with me and watch."

A prejudice is having your mind so made up facts won't change it.

Well, the warden got up in the boat with him and they took off out in the middle of the river. The game warden said, "All right, Claud, I'm going to see how you catch all these fish when can't nobody else catch any."

Claud raised the lid on the boat seat, got a big long stick of dynamite, lit the fuse on it, let it go down kind of short, drew back, and chunked it. Blam! Lots of big catfish came belly up, and Claud was just whipping them out by the tubful.

The game warden screeched, "Boy, that's against the law. You can't do that. Don't you know you are breaking the law?"

Well, Claud lit another big stick of dynamite and handed it to the game warden. The game warden took that stick of dynamite and said, "You idiot, this is against the law; you can't do this."

Claud said, "You gonna sit there and argue—or fish?"

Marcel was always trying to get into a business where he could make a profit and not have to work as hard as he did hauling pulpwood. He went into the moving business one time with a partner named James Lewis—Marcel Ledbetter Moving Company. He borrowed some money and got a few trucks. One day the phone rang.

"Mr. Ledbetter will you move a grand piano for me?"

"Yes, ma'am."

They got to this three-story house with a big bay window on the second floor. The lady wanted to move the piano out of the bay-windowed room and onto the ground below. Marcel got up to the second floor and there didn't seem to be any way. He couldn't see how to get that piano down. But finally he said, "I know what I'll do." He got on top of the house with a big two-by-six and stuck it out over the top of the house, put a block and tackle up there, brought the end down into the bay window, and tied a rope around the piano. James Lewis and the other hand went up to the second floor ready to ease the piano out the window. Marcel, down on the sidewalk, wrapped the rope around his wrist.

"All right, now. Y'all be careful. Shove her down real easy. Ah'm gonna ease it down," Marcel yelled up to them.

They eased the piano out the window and just as it left the ledge and started down, Marcel went flying upwards, yanked off his feet by that rope around his arm. He passed the piano about

A dedicated fan shared his raccoon with me at Fan Fair. (Photo by Beth Gwinn)

halfway up and then the piano hit the sidewalk and burst into a thousand pieces; splinters covered the whole street.

Marcel's head hit that pulley at the top, and down he came flat on his back, right on top of all that busted piano—knocked him unconscious. James Lewis ran down the steps. "Marcel, Marcel, are you all right? Speak to me."

Marcel opened his eyes and said, "Why should I speak to you? I just passed you twice up there and you didn't say nothin' to me."

Uncle Versie Ledbetter was a great fellow. I just loved him; he was Marcel's daddy. One day Uncle Versie went to the auction barn when I was growing up and bought a horse, paid fifty dollars for it, and took it home. A month later, Mr. De-Laughter went by Uncle Versie's house and saw the horse. Uncle Versie had currycombed him, cut his mane off, and got all the cockleburs out of his tail. It was a fine-looking horse.

Mr. DeLaughter said, "Uncle Versie, is that the same horse you bought at the sale barn for fifty dollars?"

"It is."

"I'll give you a hundred for it."

"Sold," said Uncle Versie.

Mr. DeLaughter kept the horse, took him home, put a bridle

Bashful Brother Oswald, one of the Smoky Mountain Boys, and I meet in Roy Acuff's dressing room to boot around some favorite topics. (Photo by Melodie Gimple)

on him and a saddle, stuck a plume between his ears. A month later Uncle Versie was by Mr. DeLaughter's house and said, "Mercy, is that the same horse?"

"That's the one."

"I'll give you $150 for it."

"Well, you can have him."

Uncle Versie took him home. He added one of those gadgets that makes a horse bow his neck when he runs and he shod the horse. That horse with his new saddle, bridle, and plume between his ears was a beautiful thing.

Mr. DeLaughter came by about a month later. "Versie, I'll buy that horse back from you. Give you fifty dollars profit just like we've been doing."

"Sold!"

About a month later, Uncle Versie went by to check on the horse.

"Where is that horse, Mr. DeLaughter," he asked.

"I sold him."

"What! Man, you ain't sold our horse?," he almost sobbed.

"Yeah, I sold him to a fellow out of Texas who paid a thousand dollars for it."

"Tell me you didn't sell our horse," he wept. "You don't understand! *Me and you both* was making a good living from that horse!"

You know even today city folks have difficulty understanding us country folks sometimes. I was walking by Uncle Ronnie's place one day down at Route 4, Liberty, Mississippi, and I saw a hog in his field with a wooden leg. I said, "Uncle Ronnie, that's a mighty fine hog you got there, but why does he have a wooden leg?"

"Oh, son, that hog's like a member of my family. When our house burned he rushed in and saved my grandmother. When little Eula was drowning in the creek, he jumped in and saved her. Just like a member of the family."

"But why does he have a wooden leg?"

"Son, when you got a hog that good you eat him only one ham at a time."

One time they called a deacons' meeting at the East Fork Church. Uncle Versie Ledbetter was up in years, and he didn't go to many deacons' meetings any more. He figured the young folks, the fifty- and sixty-year-olds, should take care of

Anytime your zeal runs ahead of your knowledge of what God wants done, you're asking for trouble.

church business. But he got word the deacons were fixing to spend some money so he got his grandson, Newgene, to take him to the meeting. The deacons got into a big discussion about buying a chandelier.

One man said, "I move we buy a chandelier for the church."

"Second the motion."

"Is there any discussion?"

Uncle Versie said, "Sir, I'd like to speak. I want all of you to know that if we go and buy a chandelier there isn't anybody in our church with enough education to spell it right when we order it from Sears and Roebuck. Then if we order the chandelier and it gets here, there's nobody in our church that knows how to play it. And what I'm real concerned about—we don't need to spend this money on a chandelier as bad as we need lights in the church!"

✉ Straight from the U.S. Mail Bag

Dear Jerry,

I have intended to write you for about a year and a half. The title of your book, *Ain't God Good*, was a source of testimony during a difficult period in my life. Before my husband died he was ill for over four years; the last two or three he spent a great deal of time in the hospital. As friends visited and expressed their empathy, "Ain't God Good" became a marvelous reply.

I have referred friends to your book as a source of strength as well as a way to be "cheered up." Thank you for this great book. May it continue to be a blessing to others as it has been to me.

Emily L. Morrow

Some People Are So Heavenly Minded, They Ain't No Earthly Good

It is not my intention to be critical of other people by having a chapter named "Some People Are So Heavenly Minded, They Ain't No Earthly Good." Friends know me to be a very conservative Christian who believes that Jesus did not even get his feet wet when He walked on the water. It has been my privilege to be an active Christian churchman for forty-six years. Occasionally, though, I get discouraged at some of my friends who write me or stop me on the road to tell me that I haven't fitted exactly into their spiritual mold. One time my manager called me and said, "Jerry, the Executive Inn in Owensboro, Kentucky, wants you to perform up there one weekend."

"Isn't that a nightclub?" I asked.

Tandy explained that Mr. Green, owner of the inn, wanted me to perform because it was the weekend the State Convention of Alcoholics Anonymous was going to meet in Owensboro. I thought it was a compliment. I performed. Some pastors of local Baptist churches hurried down after the concert and said, "We're *so* glad you performed, because you are an entertainer we can bring our families to hear."

Just a few days later, however, a state Baptist paper took me to task, indicating how wrong I was for appearing there. The article quoted me as having once said I would never perform where alcohol was sold. Well, I'd never make a statement like that. You couldn't even stay at a hotel if you said that. And I try not to be *of* the world, but I'm *in* the world. In some cities you can't even buy groceries if you don't want to be around alcohol because it's for sale on the next counter.

✧ ✧ ✧

If you can get paid for doing what you love to do, you're mighty fortunate.
(Photo by Melodie Gimple)

Much was said recently about a friend of mine who appeared on national television praying, "Lord, let the storm hit somewhere else, don't let it hit me." Well, nobody asked me my opinion on that and I didn't give it, but my old Route 4-Liberty-Mississippi-Baptist-Christian upbringing can't quite understand how a person could say, "Lord, let the storm hit somebody else, don't let it hit me." Wouldn't it be better to pray, "Lord, a hurricane is headed toward me and mine. I pray that it will turn, head out to sea and not hurt anybody. But if it's got to hit inland, I pray it hits me and mine; and Lord, please give me strength to handle it." Now I believe that's Christian. I really do.

Not too long ago I got a phone call from the chairman of a pulpit committee wanting to visit the First Baptist Church in Yazoo City and hear my preacher. Now that chairman was a nice fellow, and he said, "Jerry, we're friends, and I wanted to call you to check and see if it would strain our friendship any if I brought a pulpit committee to hear your preacher." I said, "Man, what are you sayin'? If my preacher leaves my church, I'm gonna cry. It's going to hurt me. I love him so much. He's been my pastor for twenty-five years, but I'll be the first one to help him move if he says the

120

Lord is calling him to go somewhere else. I do not want a pastor preaching to me who is not in the confines of the will of God. You bring your pulpit committee; you come right on and you listen to him; and you let the Spirit move you one way or the other, and whatever way the Spirit moves my preacher, I'll pray for him and wish him well."

"Fine, Jerry, that's wonderful. How are you doing?"

"Man, I'm exhausted. I've never been so tired in all my life."

"Oh? What in the world has caused you to be so tired?"

"I been out raising money all day."

"Oh, what are you raising money for?"

"I'm raising money to pay for this sex change operation my preacher is fixing to have."

All I could hear on the telephone on the other end of the line was deep breathing.

66 The Jerry Clower the Pierces know in the late 1980s is the same Jerry Clower we knew in the late 1940s—warm, personable, humorous and above all a genuine Christian. (Homerline remains the same, too, a gentle lady, indeed.)

Perhaps I relate to Jerry Clower so well because I was born and reared on a "pea-patch farm" in southeast Neshoba County, Mississippi, and lived a life similar to Jerry's.

After World War II, many veterans found themselves at Mississippi State University. We lived in converted barracks the college provided for $24/month furnished, including an icebox (not a refrigerator). We formed lifelong friendships in that setting. Although we had practically no money, few clothes, and very little food, everybody shared whatever they had with their neighbors. On Sunday afternoons, a lot of us would migrate to the Clowers front lawn to enjoy entertainment for free that people pay money to see and hear today.

We had a ball. We are so glad to know the Clowers and to have shared a part of their lives. **99**

Robert and Catherine Pierce
Mississippi State friends

The Hitchhiker

The funniest things in the world actually happen. When I was a student at Mississippi State University, a traveling man got sick and died at Reform, Alabama. A hearse from Mississippi went to pick him up. The two fellows driving that hearse headed back to Mississippi but decided they would stop at a truck stop and get something to eat. The driver of the hearse stopped by the cashier's desk to pay the check and the fellow riding with him went on outside saying, "I'll see you in a moment."

When he got outside, there stood a hitchhiker wanting to ride with them.

"There ain't no place for you to ride. There ain't nothing back there except a jump seat and if you rode back there, you'd have to ride with a dead man."

"I don't care. I need to get home. I'll ride anywhere."

"All right. Get on up in the back."

The driver came out and got behind the steering wheel. He didn't know about the hitchhiker in the back and his partner was sound asleep by that time. The driver cranked up that big Cadillac hearse and went cruising down the highway in the still of the night, looking at the full moon through the windshield, doing eighty miles an hour and this hand came through the curtain, grabbed him by the shoulder, and a voice said, "Buddy, is it all right to smoke back here?"

"Dancing with Who Brung Ya"

L oyalty is a word some people don't understand. Darryl Royal, former great coach at the University of Texas, is credited with saying, "You ought to dance with who brung ya." I agree. We need to be loyal in every phase of our lives. Years ago I was listening to a talk show out of Baton Rouge and somebody called in to the LSU head football coach and said, "Who was that knucklehead who missed the field goal at the end of the game?" And the LSU coach replied, "One of the young men I coach, and we both are going to try to do better next time."

I wish there was some way to infuse Marine Corps kind of loyalty into the church. If my denomination, the Southern Baptist Convention, could carry out church functions with the enthusiastic loyalty the Marine Corps carries out its goals, we would win the world to the Lord in about two weeks.

I had the privilege of staying on a marine base for three days while cutting a live album, "An Officer and a Ledbetter," at Camp Lejeune Marine Base in North Carolina. I've never seen so many good manners exhibited. "Good mornin', Sir." "How are you, Sir?" "Hello, Sir," "Can we help you, Sir?"

The sergeant who was my host left his office one day to get us some coffee, and I got to reading various plaques and looking at pictures on the wall. One of them had to do with the sergeant's receiving the Navy Cross. Now that is the second highest honor the United States of America gives to servicemen. I read the commendation hanging on the wall describing this sergeant's rescue of his mortally wounded commanding officer in Viet Nam. He ran through machine-gun fire to do so. And when this sergeant reached him, the captain's first words were, "Prop me in a shooting position." Now, folks, my first thought probably would have been, "Maybe you can hide me good enough with that brush over there

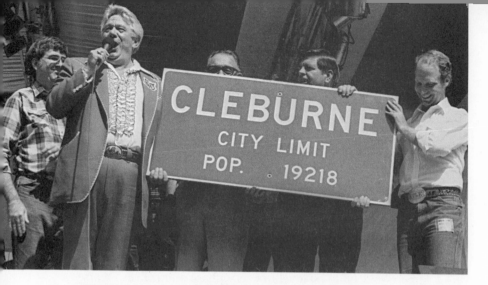

When I recorded my 1983 album live from Cleburne, Texas, the town gave me a city-limits sign and a continuous roll of appreciative laughter. I do love small towns! (Photo by Beth Gwinn)

so when those folks come by here they won't find me, and I can get out alive and get back home." But, no, here was an officer of the United States Marine Corps so loyal to the corps that his dying words were "Prop me up."

If we could get that kind of loyalty into our everyday lives to carry out good things, it would make a difference.

Some companies have inspired this kind of loyalty. I'm partial to Delta Airlines, because Delta had its birth among agricultural people trying to figure out a way to kill boll weevils and other cotton insects. They crop dusted. From that beginning grew Delta and two very different tales of company loyalty.

When Sue, my daughter, and her husband, Ken Hall, were on their honeymoon, they flew from Florida via Delta Airlines to Colorado to join a church group of college-aged young people on a ski trip. All went splendidly until changing planes at the Dallas/Ft. Worth airport. Suddenly, a man appeared in the crowd, pulled a pistol and grabbed a ten-year-old boy around the neck. Shooting his pistol in the air, he began screaming demands. The outcome was a happy one, though details of the rescue are not clear to me. Most vividly I remember Sue's call home when it was all over.

"Daddy," she said, her voice trembling, "You've been bragging about Delta Airlines, and you have been doing right. They were marvelous. One Delta man yelled to all us people in the section, 'Everybody get down.' We got down and then he put his body between me and the man with the pistol. And all the other Delta folks came running to the concourse; they locked arms and made a shield. The only way that crazed man could have shot one of Delta's customers was to have killed a Delta Airline employee first."

My other Delta story embodies a feeling of responsibility and loyalty to company roots. The Delta annual stockholders' meeting is traditionally held in Monroe, Louisiana, at a bank where the organizers first met to discuss the possibility of creating an airline.

"Any new business?" the moderator queried at the appropriate time.

"Sir, I'd like to propose we move our annual stockholders' meeting from Monroe, Louisiana, and rotate it to various cities—San Francisco, Atlanta, New York, Boston, Raleigh, Durham, Miami . . . ."

A second well-dressed man got up.

"I want to move the meeting out of Monroe, and I represent eighty thousand shares of Delta Airlines stock. I'm voting to move it."

Then, a distinguished-looking man in his seventies, wearing a beautiful suit, rose from his chair, smiled at everybody, and said,

Homerline's Squash

6 medium yellow squash
1 medium onion
2 eggs
Bacon drippings

Cook squash and onion until tender. Mash vegetables. Add eggs and bacon drippings. Put in baking dish and bake at 425 degrees for 30 minutes.

125

Folks don't have many friends. If you've got one, you need to love him and cultivate him.

"My name is Bernard W. Biedenharn. I represent five hundred eighty thousand shares of Delta Airlines stock. I'd like to welcome you people back to Monroe next year." Mr. Biedenharn's loyalty is still tied to the company's roots. Did you know, Mr. Biedenharn's daddy, Joe Biedenharn, was the first man ever to bottle a Coca-Cola? He put the Coca-Cola in bottles and sold it from a little push cart down the streets of Vicksburg. His old candy company has now been restored and it's a great tourist attraction on the main street in Vicksburg, Mississippi. That's just an interesting sidelight for your next trip-making plans.

Sometimes we may let our zeal to be loyal run ahead of our knowledge of the facts, and we use it for bad in place of good. Once I appeared on the top-rated TV morning talk show in Chattanooga, Tennessee. When I got to the studio, the makeup folks told me, "Now, Jerry, yesterday the co-host, a woman, got to crying because the host of the show was really down on young men seeking amnesty."

You see, this was before President Carter said he would grant amnesty to those young men who had fled to Canada during the Viet Nam war. The TV host had immediately declared on the air, "Anybody who's seeking amnesty ought to be lined up against a wall and shot."

Another day had dawned and there I was being introduced as a Grand Ole Opry star from Yazoo City, Mississippi. I hardly sat down before the host said, "Now, Jerry, I know you don't believe in amnesty, and you will agree with me. Don't you think all young men who fled to Canada ought to be lined up against a wall and shot?" I said, "Sir, are you talking about your boy or my boy?"

There was a pause. I said, "Because if you're talking about my boy, and my boy has been told for four years by his college professors that the Congress of the United States doesn't even have guts enough to declare war, then why should he get involved in a war that this country acts like it doesn't want to win? And they have so swayed the mind of my young son that he's gullible enough to believe all of this and maybe he fled to Canada. Now, the word *amnesty* is distasteful to me. I hate it. Had I been of age I would have fought in the Viet Nam war. It would have just been my nature to have done that. But to look back on it now, if the United States Congress didn't have guts enough to declare war, I can see where some young men would say, 'Hey, what's goin' on?' Sir, if you're talking about my son up in Canada (based on the circumstances just described), and the war is now over and my son walks to the Canadian border and says, 'Daddy, I wanna come home,' I would appreciate it if the United States Government would work it out to

Ralph Hacker interviewed me over Lorimar Sports Network during a Southeastern Conference basketball series. Hacker, color announcer for Kentucky Network, covers all the University of Kentucky's basketball and football games.

let him do so. But if you're talkin' about *your* son, I think he ought to be lined up against the wall and shot."

Sometimes you got to get your perspective right before exhibiting loyalty. That's the truth.

✧ ✧ ✧

I think some of the most loyal people in the world are country music fans. Just recently I got off an airplane at Raleigh/Durham airport and an old boy ran up to me. Clenching his fists and turning red in the face, he said to me, "Jerry, did they ever catch them sorry scoundrels who busted up Mr. Bill Monroe's mandolin?" He was ready to fight!

And then, just the other day, I got a taxi to the airport. My driver was a real Jerry Clower fan. As I handed him the money he looked at me and with much sadness said, "Mr. Clower, if I owned this cab, you wouldn't owe me a dime. I love you." Now that's loyalty. I believe in it; I try to live it. I recommend you do, too.

 Straight from the U.S. Mail Bag

Dear Jerry,

All Christians are proud of your stand for Christian principles and high moral standards in a world where Satan is having a field day. God only made one Jerry Clower. I just wish we had a few thousand clones like you. We love you.

Respectfully,
Tommy Parker

I Love Small Towns

Man I love small towns. There live the people who made me what I am. I cut one album at Cleburne, Texas, and another at Starke, Florida. My schedule always contains firm commitments in towns like Port Lavaca, Freeport, Burnet, Columbia, Ava, Dyersburg, Wynne, Searcy, Waynesville, Greenville, Statesville, Laurel, Hiawassee, Carlinville, Bonifay . . . I love small towns.

I know big towns. I went to one the other day, checked into one of them super dynawhopping, mo-jodooley, whimdiddly hotels. I got out of my limousine and walked into the lobby of this beautiful edifice. Every bellhop had a claw-hammer tailcoat. I walked up to the registration desk and there was a good-looking lady ready to register me. She was a fancy woman with gold chains around her neck, diamonds on her fingers sparkling as she played a console computer. Boy, she was doing it. But that woman had so much green paint on her eyelids I thought her gallbladder had busted.

I love Fan Fair crowds. They come from all over the fifty states and sometimes spend a whole year anticipating the next Fan Fair in Nashville. Their enthusiasm is fantastic.
(Photo by Beth Gwinn)

129

So You Want to Be a Star

People ask me all the time, "Jerry, will you help me? Here's a song I wrote. What should I do with it. I want to be in show business."

Well, I really don't have any rule of thumb. I do have some warnings. Go slowly. Be thorough. Be sure you want to be a star. Think about the discipline being an entertainer requires. If you are a parent pushing a child up the show business ladder, don't. That may be one of the greatest forms of child abuse I have ever seen.

Bill Monroe (left) is known as the father of bluegrass music, and Grant Turner (right) has been the Grand Ole Opry announcer since 1945. Monroe was inducted into the Opry in 1939.

Don't pay anyone a large sum of money to cut a record for you. If you really have talent, a record company will find you. Make your own cassette tape and peddle that cassette, or try to get it to somebody in a position to help you.

Now if you think of that *somebody* as *connections*, mine were all related to my job—selling fertilizer. As a representative of Mississippi Chemical Company, I addressed agricultural groups all the time; speaking in public came naturally to me and I did it all the time. It was part of my job. Once or twice I recorded my own speeches. Another time a friend from Lubbock, Texas, Big Ed Wilkes, recorded my stories because he just liked to hear them. Big Ed was farm director for KFYO in Lubbock, and he believed so much in the laughter-producing power of those stories, he invited a group of friends in, had the event catered, and asked me to tell some stories. Bud Andrews, another friend, and Big Ed recorded that event. I sold eight thousand of those discs just by mentioning at my fertilizer-selling gatherings that some of my stories were available on record. Not only that, but Ed Wilkes knew the farm directors of other radio stations, and he sent each one a copy of the record.

John McDonald, then farm director at WSM in Nashville, played it and gave the record to Grant Turner, Grand Ole Opry's perennial announcer.

Promoter Jim Clemments heard my record over KIKK in Houston. He talked with Joe Sutton, an artist-procurer for Universal City, California, and asked him to locate Jerry Clower, "because," he said, "he could sell ten thousand albums in the Houston area." That got my album a major record label—Music Corporation of America, MCA Records.

Meanwhile, I was still selling fertilizer and not about to stop, so you see why I'm not the best one to ask about becoming a star. I was just focusing on doing the best I could with what I had—and that included telling stories.

The best piece of advice I can give someone wanting to be in show business is do the best you can with what you've got—and do it today. Work hard. If it's meant to be, it will happen.

If things start to happen, get a good manager. Tandy Rice of Top Billing rescued me from total chaos after a couple of TV appearances prompted a deluge of phone calls and mail. He was the

The success of my business relationship with Tandy Rice is simple. He knows me so well he knows what I dream about when I put my big old head on the pillow every night. Tandy tells me he wakes up each morning thinking, "What can I do for Jerry Clower today?" I've left everything about the business in Tandy's hands since Day One . . . and all on a handshake. I'm grateful for all he's done.

best thing that could have happened to my career as a professional entertainer. He's managed my career for years, and I am grateful. I have nothing to do with my show business career. The only thing I do is show up and do what Tandy asks me to do. Now, you've got to have complete trust in the folks running your show business career, and the best way I know to convince people that I have trust in my management is to point out that since Day One I have had no other management than Tandy Rice's. Millions of dollars have been sent back and forth between his agency and Yazoo City, and we've done every bit of this on a handshake. I not only trust him, but I love him and he loves me.

When I first backed into show business, I was such a greenhorn. MCA Records called me, "Jerry, you just broke into *Billboard* with a bullet."

"You're crazy," I said. "I haven't broken into anywhere and I know I haven't used a bullet."

"Jerry, you don't understand, your album has just been listed in the country charts in *Billboard Magazine*. It's got a little star by it meaning it will move up higher. Folks in show business call that little star a bullet." It did move up higher and I understand all that stuff now, but I don't need to understand it; I've got a man looking after my show business career. All I have to do is just function and perform. And I've got a lady in Yazoo City, Mississippi, who handles the logistics of buying airline tickets, renting cars, and putting me here and there. It's just a smooth, sweet, operation.

One final bit of advice I can give is that it's good to be pretty dad-blamed sure you have talent before you get in too deep. I remember the first time I really felt as if I did. Early in my career with Tandy I was playing to an audience in a Tennessee state park between Nashville and Knoxville. My date at the park—and I love state parks—was not under the best of conditions. About twenty-five couples had gathered in front of an outdoor stage. There was no amplification for my voice, and so I just had to boom my stories at them with the strength of my own vocal chords. After it was over, Tandy and I got back in the car and he said, "Performing to twenty-five couples and exhibiting a zeal to make them laugh just as if you were performing to twenty-five thousand . . . doing it without benefit of a microphone and making them love it . . . I don't know whether you know it or not, but that is called *talent*." That was good to hear. That was the first time I ever had the feeling *in my heart* that somebody else had confidence in me. From that day forward I was booked on concerts, rodeos, and fairs.

You want to be in show business? I can't give you five easy rules. I can only tell you what worked for me, and if I've helped you, then I'm glad.

✉ Straight from the U.S. Mail Bag

Jerry dear,

The response to *Portrait of America: Mississippi* outside of Mississippi has been extraordinary. People are deeply moved and have changed their views of Mississippians considerably. We've already been nominated by several film festivals, and TBS is lining up the show for many more.

I cannot thank you enough for the genuine effort and great talent you gave to this project. I believe, as does everyone who has seen the Clower portrait, that the mixture of emotion and humor is a powerful instrument of healing.

Warmly,
Merle Worth
Producer of *Portrait of America: Mississippi*, TBS

Runaway Truck

I want to salute the truckers of America. I tell my daughters whenever they get out on the highway and the car breaks down to flag down a trucker; he will help them.

Ardell and Burnell Ledbetter took a test one time to be truckers. They took the driving part of it and said they "done good." The man giving the test working with the highway patrolman said, "Y'all come to such-and-such a building on such-and-such a day, and you can take the written and oral part of this truck-driving test."

Ardell and Burnell showed up, took the written test and passed it. Then the highway patrolman said, "Now I'll give you the oral part of it."

He said, "Ardell Ledbetter, let's say you're driving this truck. You top a hill; down at the bottom you see blue lights flashing, hear sirens blowing. Bodies are lying beside the road. There isn't anything for you to do but take to the ditch. Now what is the first thing you're going to do when you pull off the shoulder and head toward the ditch? What's the first reaction you will have when you leave the road?"

Ardell said, "I'm gonna wake up Burnell."

"My goodness, man, you're going to wake up your brother, Burnell. Why?"

He said, "Burnell ain't never seen no bad truck wreck before."

The Ledbetters

I've learned a lot from being associated with the Ledbetter family. They keep a lot of good traditions alive. I remember when I was a little boy, everything in the community revolved around the country store. You could go to the country store and find out who was fishing or hunting; then the next day you could find out what they caught or killed by going back there. One time Marcel Ledbetter came by the store and he'd been quail hunting. Mr. Duvall Scott, who ran the store, said, "Marcel, how many quail did you kill?" Marcel said, "Fifteen." A fellow sitting there warming his hands by the old potbellied stove looked up and said, "Marcel, you killed fifteen quail? I bet you shot 'em settin' in the ground." Marcel said, "Can they fly?"

Mr. Duvall Scott didn't have very many vices, but one was horse racing. He loved to go to McComb, Mississippi, and catch the City of New Orleans train down to New Orleans and go to the horse races, pick out a horse, and bet a few dollars. One time he went to New Orleans. He was betting on the horses and he lost his money. He went up to the office of the people who run the race track, got some checks cashed, and he lost that money, too. Well, he caught the City of New Orleans northbound and came back home to the East Fork community. He was waiting on customers in his country store when he bragged about how he had stopped payment on the checks he wrote in New Orleans. He said, "Them ole gamblers have got plenty of money." Yes, Duvall bragged everywhere that he'd stopped payment on those checks and beat those gamblers out of that money.

In about two weeks a big black A-model limousine came pulling up to Mr. Duvall Scott's store. He saw it was a Louisiana car. Two fellows were in there with fancy suits on and big hats with the brims pulled down over their eyes. Duvall hid in the storm pit. His wife told them that he wasn't there.

"Well, we're goin' to hunt him." So they hunted him by the day and every time they'd come by the store, Mr. Duvall Scott would be hidden in the storm pit. Well, those fellows took to the road and decided to get some of the neighbors to tell where Duvall was. They drove up to the Versie Ledbetter farm, and there was Marcel plowing one mule, and Uncle Versie plowing another, plowing out a late patch of June corn. Marcel pulled out to the end of the row just as this big black A-model limousine stopped, and that New Orleans hoodlum got out and walked up to the fence and said, "Hey, boy."

"You talkin' to me?"

"Yea, I'm talkin' to you. Do you know where Duvall Scott is?"

"I do not know where Duvall Scott is," Marcel said.

And the fellow from New Orleans said, "Them's mighty crooked rows of corn you plowin' there."

"We can grow as much corn on a crooked row as you can on a straight one."

"Well, your corn looks mighty yellow."

The duties of a corporate spokesman require making commercials. Above, we get the job done at one of the many Sonny's Real Pit Bar B-Q family restaurant franchises.

"We planted yellow corn."

"Well, there ain't much difference between you and a fool is there, boy?" the city fellow said.

Marcel said, "Nothin' but this fence right here."

About that time Uncle Versie pulled out to the end of the row. And that city fellow hollered, "Ole man, do you know where Duvall Scott is?"

"I don't know where he is, but if I did know, I wouldn't tell you. You a city dude comin' here tryin' to hurt our storekeeper and he's the only storekeeper we got in this community. Y'all leave here and leave him alone."

Well, the city dude reached up under the coat he was wearing and pulled out one of those owl-head pistols, thumb-cocked it, and shot down at Uncle Versie's feet and said, "Ole man Ledbetter, you don't know where Duvall Scott is. Let's see if you know how to dance." And pow, he shot. Pow! Pow! Pow! Pow! And Uncle Versie counted the times that pistol shot and when those shots added up to six, Uncle Versie walked around the old mule, Della, and he had a sawed-off shotgun fastened on the hangs of that mule's gear. He kept it there to shoot blackbirds out of the corn. He lifted the sawed-off shotgun, walked around and stuck it under the chin of that city fellow, thumb-cocked it, both barrels, a sawed-off shot-

It was General MacArthur who said if he had one crucial battle to fight, he'd want to fight it with athletes. There's a great lesson in winning and paying the price to achieve something.

gun, and he got that man back over the hood of his A-model limousine and said, "Now, city fellow, I just wonder if you've ever had the privilege of kissin' a fifteen hundred-pound green-lip, bad-breath mule right square-dab in the mouth?" And this city fellow said, "No, sir, but I have always wanted to."

One of the traditions the Ledbetters kept alive while I was growing up with them was sitting up with the dead. Back in those days, if you were grown you could just walk around and kinda do like you pleased. But the minute you died they assigned about six or more folks to watch you. They sat up with the dead.

Not too long ago, they was sitting up with a dead fellow out at the funeral home, and at ten o'clock the funeral director came walking in and said, "Ladies and gentlemen, this funeral home is closed. It'll open back up at nine o'clock in the morning." I happened to be sitting there and I said, "Well, hallelujah, isn't this wonderful? Let the funeral-home folks sit up with the dead."

Everybody left but Uncle Versie, and he told the funeral home director, "Sir, now I realize that this is your business and you've said you was going to close the funeral home, but we've got an old tradition out there where I come from, and we kinda sit up with the dead. Now you go ahead and lock that door, but I'm going to leave two of my boys here to sit up with the dead man the rest of the night. I'd just feel better if they did that." Ardell and Marcel had been sitting there about an hour, and Ardell could look out the window and see the neon lights on a beer joint down the road, and he looked at Marcel and smacked his lips.

"I believe I'll step down there and get us somethin' to drink."

"Nu-huh, I ain't stayin' here with him by myself," Marcel said. "I'll step down there and get us somethin' to drink." And Ardell said, "Nu-huh, I ain't stayin' here with him by myself." They sat there a while and they got to thinking how wonderful it would be if they could go down and get something to drink; their mouths were dry as cotton. They decided they'd go down to the beer joint and just take the dead man with 'em. They got him up out of the casket, and they walked on each side of him and they let his feet kinda' bounce in the road—looked like he was walking with them.

Guitarist, vocalist, and song writer Bobby Bare and I team up for a Music City News *awards show.* (Photo by Don Putnam)

They walked into the beer joint, went over to the counter, stood him up straight, put one of those three-legged stools behind his back, and he stood there just as straight as he could. That dead fellow was the best-dressed man in the beer joint. Ardell and Marcel were standing on each side of him participating in the beverages served at this joint. About that time a fight broke out. Pretty soon you could hear the sirens blowing and officers of the law coming to break up the fight.

Well, in the melee, somebody hit the dead fellow right on the point of his chin and knocked him sprawling out in the middle of the floor. Ardell fell down and put his arms under the dead man's head and went to screaming, looked up and pointed into the face of the man who had hit the dead man and said, "You killed him. You killed him. I saw you when you killed him." About that time the sheriff came busting through the door and heard what Ardell said, and he handcuffed the man who started screaming, "No, sir, sheriff. No, sir. I ain't goin' to lie about it. I did hit that fellow, but it was self-defense. He pulled a pocket knife on me."

140

M arcel Ledbetter has a son named Tater. Tater loves to go to the lumberyard where Marcel hauls pulpwood. The man who owns the yard also owns a little moped-motor-scooter-bicycle thing. While they unload the pulpwood, the manager of the yard allows Tater to ride that moped.

One day Tater zoomed out through a hole in the fence and got out on the hard road even though he'd been told never to leave the yard. Just as Tater pulled up to a red light, a beautiful Mercedes pulled up alongside of the moped and stopped. Tater leaned over, tried to look inside this beautiful car, put his nose up on the window, and the man behind the steering wheel spooled the window down.

Tater said, "Oh, mister, this is the most beautiful car I have ever seen in all of my life. Ohhh, smell that upholstery. Oh, how beautiful. How fast will it go?"

"One hundred eighty."

"One hundred eighty, ohhh, ain't you somethin' to have a car like this."

Well, about that time the light turned green, and the man decided he would impress Tater even more. He just scratched off with

❝ I worked with Jerry from the very first record. He is a deeply religious man with a great attitude toward life and a tremendous amount of energy. He takes everything the way it comes and makes the best of it. If you see Jerry in a fight with a bear, help the bear. Jerry won't need it. ❞

Chic Doherty
V.P., retired, MCA Records

the tires burning and got up to about a hundred miles an hour. He looked in the rearview mirror and here came a speck behind him. And he got to looking and he said, "Good gracious," and about that time—whooom—something passed him. And he said, "Good gracious alive, that looks like that little old boy on the moped." And about that time—whoooom—that little boy came back again. And the fellow said, "It was. It was that little old boy on the moped. How in the world is he doing that?" About that time the fellow saw that speck coming again, and there was Tater and the moped— wham—it hit right into the back of the Mercedes. The man got the Mercedes stopped, jumped out and went back to where Tater was lying in amongst a crumpled up, busted up moped, and the man said, "Are you hurt? Are you hurt? My goodness, young man, you were so courteous and such a nice young fellow, I hope you're not hurt. Is there anything in the world I can do for you?" And Tater said, "Yessir, you can unhook my suspenders from your side-view mirror."

I grew up with Clovis, Marcel Ledbetter's youngest brother. Clovis loved to eat so well he would just steal a chicken or a goat every now and then. One time he got arrested for stealing a sheep, and they put him in jail.

A lawyer visited him there and said, "Clovis, they have caught you, son, isn't any way you can get out of jail unless you hire a good

142

lawyer like me to represent you. I can get you out for fifty dollars."
Now this was a smart lawyer, a fancy fellow. He had a hairdo that
looked like a milking machine had been sucking on it.

Clovis said, "Man, I ain't got no fifty dollars."

"Well, you can work it out for me. Come over to my place and
cut the grass and clean the yard."

"All right, I sure don't want to go to Parchman, the state peni-
tentiary in Mississippi."

When Clovis Ledbetter was in the courtroom for the trial, the
lawyer told him, "Clovis, you do exactly as I tell you and I'll get
you out of this."

The District Attorney started by asking, "Mr. Clovis Ledbetter, on the night of April 13 did you steal a sheep?"

Clovis said, "Baaaaa!"

He asked Clovis another question and got the same "Baaaaa!"

The judge looked down sternly at Clovis and said, "You answer that man's questions. What do you mean making that noise?"

Clovis looked at the judge and said, "Baaaaa!"

The judge took his hammer and hit the desk, said, "Get that
idiot out of here; he's crazy. Case dismissed!"

Well, the next day the lawyer went and hunted up Clovis and
wanted his fifty dollars; Clovis looked at him and said, "Baaaaa!"

✉ Straight from the U.S. Mail Bag

Dear Jerry,
    I know from watching my TV, everything is going great with you. I have enclosed a little poem you might be interested in. I wrote it several years ago from an old anecdote my father used to tell.

Sincerely,
Bert Jenkins

Maw, I Want A Piece Of Chicken

The grown-ups at the table ate;
The preacher had his false teeth clickin'.
The little boy was told to wait.
"Hey, Maw, I want a piece of chicken."

"Keep still now, Son, you know the rule.
You young'uns wait—take second pickin'."
The smell of chicken made him drool.
"Please, Maw, I want a piece of chicken."

"You hush and let the preacher eat,
Or, hear me, you will get a lickin'."
The boy looked down then at his feet.
"But, Maw, I want a piece of chicken."

The chicken slowly disappeared.
"Don't like to waste," the preacher said.
The last piece gone—just as he feared.
"Hey, Maw, I want to go to bed."

Editor's Note: According to Jerry, Mr. Jenkins is the best high school basketball coach in the South. He works as Head Coach at Gulfport High School.

The Burning Building

I grew up on Route 4, Liberty, Mississippi, a small-town county seat with a volunteer fire department. It was the middle of the summer—big drought, no water. Everybody knew if a building caught on fire it was gone, because we just couldn't draw up enough water fast enough to put out a fire.

One Saturday evening a building caught fire. A crowd gathered with its arms folded, squalling, watching that building burn. About that time Uncle Versie Ledbetter and Aunt Pet came by in their old truck with all their young'uns. Ardell, Burnell, Raynell, W. L., Lynell, Odell, Udell, Marcel, Claud, Newgene and Clovis were all hanging on that old truck.

Everybody heard them coming, fenders rattling, blop, bablop, bablop. The crowd parted because the truck was coming so fast. It ran right up on the sidewalk and right on up into the middle of the fire. The Ledbetters jumped off, took off their overalls and went to flopping and stomping the fire out. Aunt Pet Ledbetter in her bonnet kept telling them, "Hey, stomp it over here, beat it out!" and they stomped that fire out! They put it slap out.

Folks cheered, "The Ledbetters are heroes. They put out the fire."

Everybody passed the hat, took up a collection, thirty-one dollars, gave the money to Uncle Versie, and said, "Sir, we love you. You are a hero. Tell us, what are you gonna buy with the thirty-one dollars?"

"The first thing I'm going to do is get the brakes fixed on that truck!"

Habits Bad and Good

Some folks have developed a habit of being mad about everything. The maddest fellow I ever heard of was riding the Panama Limited, the main line of mid-America, the Illinois Central Railroad that runs from New Orleans to Chicago and back. Fastest train in the world. When I was a boy, a man stepped on the bottom step of that train in Mississippi, turned around to kiss his mama goodbye, and kissed a bull in the mouth at Hammond, Louisiana. When that train takes off, it takes *off!*

Well, a traveling salesman got on the train in Chicago, headed south. "Porter," he said, "I am afraid to go to my roomette to sleep because I may not wake up in time to get off this train to make my calls in the morning at Winona, Mississippi." The porter said, "Sir, that's why I'm on the train—to wake you up. I will not only wake you up, I will also hand you a good hot cup of coffee. You'll be bright-eyed and ready to get off to make your calls in Winona, Mississippi." The traveling salesman replied, "Sir, you don't understand. I'm hard to wake up. My metabolism doesn't get going 'til I've had about eight cups of coffee. If I am asleep when you call me in the morning and I don't answer you, and you put your hands on me and shake me, I have been known to come up fighting, and if I come up fighting you'll say 'the heck with me' and won't put me off the train."

The porter said, "I've had this job thirty-seven years. I deal with people like you every day. Lots of folks are hard to wake up. I don't care how much fighting you do. I don't care how much resistance you give me. If you tell me to put you off the train, I'll put you off." Well, the man woke up the next morning and he had slept well. Real well. He raised the drape to look out of the window and the train was sitting still. A sign on the depot said "McComb, Mississippi." That's two hours south of Winona. That man got so mad he threw a fit; all the veins stood out on the side of his neck, and he turned blood red. The man was so mad he slapped a fellow down on the train. The police came aboard and drug him off the train. The railroad folks called the president of the Illinois Central Railroad and they said, "Mr. President, we've got a man down here who's so mad he's a maniac. How do you want us to handle him?" The president of the railroad said, "It's your fault you got him this mad. You did not wake him up so you give him whatever money he lost because you didn't put him off the train at Winona, and you put him on the next northbound back to Winona immediately. Furthermore, hurry up about it. Calm the man down and tell him when the next northbound is due back to Winona, but get your train out of McComb headed south toward New Orleans right now." Well, they got the man calmed down enough to board the next northbound train to Winona. And the engineer pulled the southbound out of McComb headed toward New Orleans. That porter reached into his pocket, got out his handkerchief and started mopping the blood and the sweat off his face where the madman had clawed him. And the porter's co-worker sitting across the aisle looked over at him and said, "You know, that sure was a mad human being." The porter sitting there wiping off his face with the

Backstage at the Opry I get to meet some of my fans. (Photo by Melodie Gimple)

handkerchief looked at his co-worker and said, "Not only mad but *the maddest* man I believe I have ever seen in my life, don't you agree?" And the porter's co-worker said, "Yeah, he was a mad fellow, but I've seen one other man in my lifetime madder than him." And the brow-mopping porter said, "Who in the world could that have been?" His co-worker said, "The man I put off in Winona this morning."

I've often wondered why, if we're going to become addicted to doing something, we can't develop good habits as well as bad. Why don't we get in the habit of going to church? Why don't we get in the habit of loving our families? Why don't we get into a habit of being on time? So, by logical deduction, we are developing habits to serve Satan more than we are developing habits to serve the Lord. I was fishing one time, catching big old slab white perch. (Now don't let me confuse anybody, in Mississippi we call this fish a white perch. In other parts of the country that fish is crappie. Down in south Louisiana, it's sacalait.) I was catching those big old slab white perch when my buddy asked me if I had a match. "Hush," I said. "You may scare off the fish. I do not have a match." That man laid his pole down in the boat, cranked up the engine, went back to shore because he said, "I'm havin' a nicotine fit, I cannot go one second longer. I've got to go and get a match." I sat on the bank approximately fifteen minutes while he went and got a box of matches. And I just had the thought, what if we had been out there fishing and my buddy had said, "Jerry, I just thought of two fellows I told the church office I would visit before tonight. Both of them are unchurched. Neither one of them knows the Lord, and, man, they're having problems. The church needs to minister to them. Take in your pole, let's go get ready to tell those people we love them and we want to help them."

If you're going to develop a habit, make it a good one!

I see people, great sports figures of our nation, big managers of baseball teams, outstanding basketball coaches, who have the habit of being superstitious. They never step on a foul line walking to the pitcher's mound because it's bad luck, or they don't wash their

Jim Ed Brown and I shared hosting duties on "Nashville on the Road" for years. Here we reminisce on "Nashville Now." (Photo © 1987 by Harry Butler, Nashville)

socks after a lucky game or they'll wear a certain suit because that brings good luck. Why can't they become addicted to saying "You win ball games by effort, dedication, training, and by preparing yourself to be the best you can"?

Thinking about people addicted to doing good; one person comes to my mind above all others. The first time I ever saw her she was sitting in an old rubber car-tire. Folks back then called it a casing. That casing was hung from a cedar tree and this little girl was inside the tire, swinging. She was very, very young. And then I don't remember seeing her again until I saw her at East Fork Consolidated School, right in the heart of Amite County, Mississippi. Her name was Homerline. I remember saying, "Who in the world would name a girl Homerline, and where in the world did they get that name?" Well, I found out she was named after her daddy, Homer Wells, and I'm real glad they named her Homerline because her daddy's middle name was Ebenezer. That would have been rough: Ebenezerline.

149

She is the most unique person I have ever known in my life, not only because of her name but also because she is one person who is addicted to the ministry of doing good. I walked down the aisle of an old country church with her at age thirteen. We became Christians together. We were baptized together. We went back to that same old church to be married on August 15, 1947. We have been happily married for forty years. If God gave me the ingredients and told me to make a woman, I'd make her exactly like Homerline. I have never known her, under any circumstances, to have a bad habit. She is addicted to her husband, Jerry Clower. She just has a habit of loving me and loving every member of her family, her children, her grandchildren, her kinfolks, and others. Anybody who knows her, I believe, will agree with what I'm saying. Here is an individual who is addicted to being a great person.

✉ Straight from the U.S. Mail Bag

Dear Jerry,

I know this is a proud day in your life, and I want to join your many friends who are offering their congratulations. I think it is about time they named something after you in Yazoo City, for it is Jerry Clower who put Yazoo City on the map.

You have been a great ambassador not only for Yazoo City but also for your home state of Mississippi, and what is in our favor, your creativity and loyalty to country music have made you one of its most respected spokesmen.

On a day such as this, it is nice to know that there are people such as you whose dedication to your God, your family, and your country is admired by everyone.

Sincerely,
Ralph Emery

The Resort Hotel

You know I'm not going to lie to you, but since I backed into show business I have been making above-average means, and I never did know how some of the more affluent folks lived. Well, not too long ago I was invited to do a show for some folks at a world famous resort hotel. Yachts were tied up in the harbor; the bellhop met me in a tall hat. He got my bags and helped me up to my room where I found some imported German chocolates on a silver tray "for Mr. Clower's benefit." The bellhop hung up my clothes, put my suitcase up, and right away I'm thinking about getting comfortable for the Nebraska–Alabama football game on television that afternoon. I got there a half-day early so I wouldn't miss it.

As I went to tip the bell man, I said, "Sir, where is the television in this room?"

"We don't have television at this hotel."

I'm excited about performing anywhere, but families are my favorite audience. I think families need to laugh together . . . and they don't have a whole lot of choice for a stand-up-talker-entertainer in today's world.

"What?" I said, "Man, they got television at those $18.88-a-night places."

"Oh, sir, you don't understand. Our guests come here not to be disturbed by television."

I said, "Well, I would hope they got sense enough to turn it off if they don't want to watch it. I'm *going* to see Nebraska and Alabama play. I done fell out with you rich folks already."

"Well, the TV room is down close to the lobby."

Now, folks, I had to dress, and what I was wanting to do was put on my loose-fitting pajamas where the air-conditioning unit could blow up this pajama leg and go down that one, and watch Bear Bryant's boys (he was still with us then) whup up on Nebraska. But I had to dress and go down to the lobby to watch the dad-blamed football game.

I was down there watching it, it's the third quarter, and the score's tied. In walked four high-society women in those little fancy frizzled britches, cute little caps on their heads, each one holding a tennis racquet. They came walking in and said, "O, sir, we're going to change the television channel."

"Ma'am?".

They said, "Oh, yes, the Slim Jim tournament is on the other station."

I said, "Ladies, I love everybody, but y'all are fixing to read big headlines in the morning paper, all the way across the page, 'Grand Ole Opry star and born-again Southern Baptist whips four women at world-famous resort hotel.'"

Gigglin' and Grinnin'

Work was hard to find in south Mississippi and one old boy had heard there was work in New York City. An old lady in the community heard about this boy going to New York hunting a job and she met him down where he was waiting for the bus. Just before the bus arrived, she explained to him, "Son, I have a boy who went to New York three months ago hunting work and I haven't heard from him. I'd appreciate it very much, should you see him up there, if you would tell him to write his mama. My son's name is John Dunn. I hope you run into him." Poor soul, she probably thought New York was about the size of Bogue Chitto, Mississippi.

The old boy finally made it to New York, he got off the bus, started down the street and spied a great big building. On the front of that building the sign said, "Dun and Bradstreet." "Well," he said, "there's old Dunn right there. I'll just go in and see if I can find John Dunn, that old woman's boy. So he walked in and asked the receptionist, "Have you got a John here?" She said, "Yeah, go straight down to the end of the hall." And he walked straight down to the end of the hall and just as he got to this door to the restroom a man came walking out. And this old boy said, "Are you Dunn?" He said, "Yes," and the old boy said, "Your mama said to write her a letter."

When I was at the one hundred seventy-fifth anniversary of the Old East Fork Baptist Church I ran into Marcel Ledbetter. I was real sad that Aunt Pet, his mama, wasn't at the anniversary celebration; Aunt Pet was in the hospital. The Baptist preacher had gone out to the hospital to visit with her. It seems she had been having some back problems, and the doctor had told her that her back was hurting because her bad teeth were putting poison in her system. Well, Aunt Pet went to the hospital and they put her to sleep and they pulled every tooth in her head. She was lying up there in her bed the next morning when the Baptist preacher came by and sat down and said, "Aunt Pet, how you

153

I guest-hosted a "Nashville Now" show for Nashville Network and my mother surprised me speechless by turning up in the audience. I think she could jump over a three-story building right this minute if she wanted to do so. She is some kind of woman! (Photo © 1987 by Harry Butler, Nashville)

feelin'?" As well as she could with no teeth she said, "I'm doing all right."

There was a bowl of peanuts sitting on the night stand by Aunt Pet's bed and this preacher would reach over and get one of those peanuts and eat it while he was visiting with Aunt Pet. It wasn't long before his visit was over and he'd eaten every peanut in the bowl. He got up and said, "Aunt Pet, I'll get back to see you in the mornin'. The church family is prayin' for ya. I'm glad you're doing well, and when I come in the morning I'll bring you some more peanuts." She said, "No, no, I can't bite 'em. My gums are so sore, I can't eat peanuts. What I do is just suck the chocolate off of 'em, and put the peanuts back in that bowl right there."

We have a preacher in Mississippi who is kind of a self-appointed preacher. He's never been off to seminary, but he's got a couple of churches where he preaches part time. The other day a highway patrolman saw this self-styled

154

preacher weaving down Highway 49, so the patrolman pulled him over and said, "Preacher, are you drinking?"

"Good gracious, alive, I wouldn't drink and drive."

"What's in that sack you're holding down there on your lap? You've got that sack kinda folded back . . . looks like you're drinking. Let me see that."

"Sir, there's water in that bottle I'm drinking."

Well, the highway patrolman reached over and got that sack and brought it up and took a whiff of it and said, "Preacher, there's wine in this bottle."

And the preacher yelled in a loud voice, "Praise God, He's done it again!"

Two mean brothers lived in a certain city in Mississippi. They were bad folks, never had anything to do with the church. One of those mean brothers died, and the other brother went to the local preacher. "If you'll preach my brother's funeral while his casket is down in front of the pulpit, if you'll get up and look over his casket at the congregation and say he was a saint, I'll give you $5,000."

"All right," the preacher said, "I'll do that. The church needs $5,000." The preacher got up and said, "Ladies and gentlemen, the man in this casket we're buryin' here today has got to be the most vile, meanest, low down-est scoundrel I have ever known in my life. But compared to his brother sitting right over there, this man was a saint."

When I was a boy growing up, folks who grew cotton had some geese known as "grassers." They would put the grassers in cotton fields in the last of April and the first part of May to eat the grass out of the cotton; it was just a seasonal thing. About that same time of year the muscadines got ripe in the woods. Some folks call muscadines "scuppernongs." Some folks call muscadines "bullaces." Whatever you call them, they are a delicious, big round purple-colored grape. (They're green until they ripen.)

Well, every time the muscadines get ripe, al¹ of the Ledbetters get their water buckets and go to the woods and pick them full. And they would make jelly or muscadine juice, and they put what they call the "plummins" in a big old barrel, pour some juice in there, and let them ferment. Now Uncle Versie was a godly man and he didn't believe in drinking so he would always stop the fermenting just before this barrel of squished-up muscadines got a lot of alcohol content in them. One day Uncle Versie and his whole family were at church and the geese got to smelling the fermenting muscadines in that barrel. They pecked at the smokehouse door and got into the smokehouse and started pecking on the barrel. They found a weak stave in the barrel and kept pecking and pecking and directly—kapoosha—all that muscadine juice come running out into the smokehouse, and the geese drank every bit of it.

When the Ledbetters got home from church, all sixteen of those geese were lying on their backs with their feet sticking straight up. Uncle Versie squalled and said, "Somebody's poisoned our geese. We can't eat them, because we don't know what killed them. But all of you get out here and pick them clean. We'll get us a featherbed mattress out of these geese." They picked those geese

Fellow MCA artist Lee Greenwood and I wait together backstage before performing at Fan Fair. (Photo by Rick Lance)

**All children have the right to a daddy . . .
rational and sound and showing his love
by the way he treats them.**

clean and threw them in the back of a wagon. Marcel took them
down to a creek fed by a cold, cold, underwater spring and threw
them all into that creek.

Marcel got back to the house and was helping everyone stuff
goose feathers into bed ticking to make a mattress when Udell Ledbetter screamed, "Look-a-yonder, look-a-yonder, look coming on
down the road." And about that time, walking up in the yard were
sixteen naked geese.

Nearly every county in the South has got an Oak Grove
Church—Baptist, Methodist, or Presbyterian. The one
I'm telling about now was an Oak Grove Methodist
Church in a southern county with a very strong women's temperance group. One Sunday in a worship service the temperance society was celebrating and one lady got up to present her case about
beverage alcohol. She had just about proved every bad thing that
had ever happened in that county was caused by liquor when she
asked, "Are there any questions?"

A young man, who looked like a student stood up and said,
"Yes, ma'am, Mrs. Anderson, how do you explain the fact that in
the Word of God the Lord Jesus turned water into wine?" And the
lady said, "Yes, and I'd a thought a lot more of Him if He hadn't
done that, too."

You small-town folks listen to what I'm going to tell you, because the number of a room I checked into once tells you how some big city folks are. Everybody's got to live somewhere, but this registration desk woman with the green eyelids sent me to Room 411. I got in there and pulled off my girdle so my old belly could wallow around and flop. I put on my loose-fitting pajamas and spraddled out. I turned on the TV; they had four channels and two of them was snowy! A hundred-twenty-five-dollar-a-night room and they hadn't discovered cable television in that big important hotel in that downtown area where millions of smart people are supposed to be.

Now you know they would look down their pious noses at me and they would say Jerry Clower lives in a hick town. I might—but we got twenty-one channels on the TV!

Well, here I am sitting in Room 411 with the TV on, all relaxed, and the phone rings. I said, "Hello."

"Would you please give me the room of Susie Q. Dampeer?"

I said, "What?"

"Isn't this 411?"

I said, "What?"

"I want you to give me the street and the number of Susie Q. Dampeer. This is Information 411, isn't it?"

66 **S**ometime in the future I expect to see Jerry Clower big on Broadway in a family-oriented production that will be just right to showcase his warm, outstanding storytelling gifts. **99**

Sam Luvullo
Executive Producer, "HeeHaw"

The Trucker and the Lady

A truck driver was standing in a line of people on a street corner waiting for his bus to arrive. A cute, female, girl-woman with a skirt that was little at the waist and little at the bottom and big in the middle was standing right in front of him. When the bus stopped and she tried to step up on the bus her skirt was so tight it caught her leg.

She eased her hand around and unzipped her zipper a little bit to give it some slack, went to step up on the bus but still couldn't get her legs far enough apart to make the step. She reached back the second time to unzip her zipper, tried again but still no luck. She reached around for the third time and unzipped it a little bit more and went to step up on the bus.

This good old truck driver behind her just armed her up, took her up in the bus, and set her down on the seat, and said, "Lady, I'll be late to work waitin' on you."

She drew back and whopped him side the head, and said, "You fresh thing, get your hands off of me!"

This old boy said, "Fresh? Lady, you just unzipped my britches three times."

The Gospel According to Marcel

The Ledbetter family has been good to me. Mostly I talk about Marcel Ledbetter; he's more my age and I know him better than the rest, but Marcel has ten brothers and sisters: Ardell, Burnell, Raynell, W. L., Lanell, Odell, Udell, Claud, Newgene, and Clovis.

Now according to Marcel's gospel, he is a free moral agent under God. Marcel would say the Bible is literally true except he's a little confused about that, because if the Bible is literally true then he feels he ought to be a wool-bearing animal with four legs, because the Bible does say that we are sheep and Jesus is the shepherd. But he believes the Bible to be true, and he takes each and every word of it seriously.

President David Stringfield of Nashville's Baptist Hospital and I had a chance to exchange some pretty good baptismal stories while filming a message about the hospital's services for out-of-town visitors.

God is the father of all Christians.

All in the family of God, regardless of class or color are brothers and sisters in Christ.

Each one should treat one another as such.

We belong to the family of the redeemed and we should make every effort in a decent manner to enlarge the family of the redeemed.

The family of God ought to speak in word and deed or, as the Bible says, "Let the redeemed of the Lord say so."

The strong should help the weak.

The preacher in the church ought to have full liberty to preach, even what the Bible says about race and race relations.

The Gospel of Marcel is simple. He believes you ought to do unto others as you want others to do unto you, and if a neighbor gets burned out, old Marcel will be the first one to drive up with a load of corn and a bushel of sweet potatoes. He'll even let you borrow one of his fresh milk cows if the fire burns up your cow.

Marcel believes he ought to give the first ten percent of every dime he makes to the local church. The gospel according to Marcel acknowledges that the lights don't burn at the church for free. It takes money.

And finally, Marcel Ledbetter believes it is a sin to be lazy. He really believes folks ought to make their living by the sweat of their brow.

When I worked as director of field services at Mississippi Chemical, a young man visited me who exemplifies Marcel Ledbetter's attitude toward seeking work. This young man was a red-headed, freckle-faced fellow who was neat and clean but not handsome at all.

"Mr. Clower," he said. "Yesterday I graduated from Mississippi State University with a degree in agriculture because I've always wanted to work for Mississippi Chemical. My father is a vocational agriculture teacher and I became acquainted with Mississippi Chemical through him. I've watched the employees of this company travel through the country calling on farmers. I know the reputation of that wonderful man who is the head of this organization, and it has been my life's ambition to work for this company.

161

Now I want you to know on the front, I'm not interested in what the salary is, all I want is an opportunity. All I want is a chance to show you I can be a good field representative for Mississippi Chemical Corporation. I'm asking you to put me on as a field representative and start me at whatever salary you want. It won't be long before I'll show you that my dedication, my promptness, my loyalty, my ability to work hard, will so impress you that the salary will take care of itself and my promotions will take care of themselves. All I want you to do, Mr. Clower, is to give me an opportunity."

"Son," I said, "stay right there in that chair. I'll be right back."

I walked down the hall into the office of the vice president in charge of sales and I said, "Mr. Jackson, for some time I've been thinking about hiring a sales trainee, putting him on the staff here in Yazoo City and training him to be a fill-in field representative. When a field representative gets sick or goes on vacation, this fellow can go work his territory. Then when someone leaves, I will have a well-trained person to move into that position."

Mr. Jackson said, "That's a good idea. You go ahead and do it."

"If this young man in my office passes the physical, I'm going to hire the sales trainee today," I said.

That young man went home about three hours later in a company car to tell his folks he had been hired as a sales trainee at Mississippi Chemical Corporation, and that young man did exactly what he said he would do. In fact, he did it better, because Mississippi Chemical couldn't keep him. With an attitude like that he moved on to other places. Today he is one of the top executives in the land department of one of the largest insurance companies in the world.

Now I have just described to you the attitude Marcel Ledbetter would have toward working and taking a job. That is the gospel according to Marcel when it comes to work.

Marcel Ledbetter also believes that there isn't anything like a good eyeball-to-eyeball talk when you have differences. Marcel would settle these differences as he saw his old daddy, Uncle Versie

Bill Mack and I co-host "Country Crossroads" for ACTS Network out of Fort Worth, Texas. Here we recall some good'uns on The Nashville Network's "Nashville Now." (Photo © 1987 by Harry Butler, Nashville)

Ledbetter, do years ago. I remember one time the cows broke out of a neighbor's field and got into our cornfield. My stepfather, my brother, my mama and I were distressed because the cows stayed in that cornfield most of the night, and just really boogered it up.

My stepfather went to the cows' owner and said, "Your cows stayed in my field all night."

"Well, I'm sorry, my cows broke through the fence. I didn't know they were in your field."

Neither one of these people called a lawyer, raised his voice, clenched his fists, or went to cussing. The man who owned the cows said, "I'll tell you what let's do. Let's go get an impartial person living in the community, a member of our church, and ask him to walk over the field to determine the damage. Then he can tell me how much corn he believes those cows ate and I will put that much corn in your corncrib."

My stepfather said, "What about Uncle Versie Ledbetter?"

"That's perfect. He's a fair-minded, straightforward, honest man. I'll go with his opinion, whatever it is."

Uncle Versie walked the cornfield, looked up and stated, "Twenty bushels is what's due."

That afternoon I saw this neighbor of ours drive up, open the corncrib door, and throw twenty bushels of corn into the crib. He turned and looked at my stepfather and said, "See you in church Sunday."

Now that is the gospel according to Marcel as to how neighbors ought to get along and how they ought to settle their differences.

Marcel Ledbetter is a devout, Bible-believing family man. He believes you ought to assemble yourselves together and worship together in a church house. But Marcel is all man; it won't do to cross him. He will physically protect his own. In fact, Marcel has been known to protect his family by whopping somebody, but then he'll kneel and pray over the whoppee.

66 Jerry Clower is one of the most delightful storytellers of our time. His warmth is infectious. **99**

Fred Russell
Vice-President, Nashville *Banner*

About Jerry Clower

Jerry Clower is genuine, always the same in his giving and loving . . . consistently up about life. As he says, "I don't go through life biting my fingernails. To claim to have God to lean on and then not do it—that's a sin."

Columnist Sid Salter said of Jerry, "He spreads joy, and the laughter he finds in us is simple." Roy Blount, Jr., says Jerry may be one of the few current Christians "whose prayers the Lord looks forward to if they are anything at all like the rest of the conversation."

Only the Lord knows how much good Jerry has done on the earth, and the two of them are pretty quiet about it. Although the on-stage Clower is full of raucous good humor and down-home philosophy, the offstage Clower is busily and quietly putting stars in his crown. If we can't see them too well it's either because we're doubled over laughing or because Jerry's good work is one area of his life bulwarked by silence.

As the book went to press, Jerry received this letter from Russell G. Davis, vice president of Engineering Associates, Inc., in Jackson, Mississippi. Davis had just received word that the Clowers would be returning to Liberty, Mississippi. Davis said he was writing to express, the best way he knew how, the way Jerry's friends felt about the news—and about him.

> A lot of water has gone down the Amite River in Clower-Ledbetter-Eubanks and God's country since native son Jerry left to fulfill a country boy's dream. He got pretty famous all over the world, made people laugh, and all along the way he kept his own standards about what was right. Now he's going back home, alive and well just as he left years ago—only wiser.
>
> Jerry, we're glad you will relive those early days, get to know again the feel of dirt, heat and sweat. Let your great heart take in all the goodness of the earth. Knowing you are at home and happy will make us who love you proud.

It is hard for me to believe I have been in this business for seventeen years. I have been blessed to be able to make a living doing what I love to do. With Homerline taking care of the family, Judy Moore attending to details of my schedule, and Tandy Rice masterminding arrangements in Nashville, "Hey, if I felt any better, I'd have to go fishing!" (Photo by Melodie Gimple)

Discography

For years I have been recording an album of stories each year. I've had to disappoint people who come up and ask which story appears on what record; I just don't remember offhand. For those of you who want to know, here's the whole truth.

JERRY CLOWER FROM YAZOO CITY MISSISSIPPI TALKIN'
MCA 33 (selections previously released on Decca album DL7-5286)
Introduction by Big Ed Wilkes
A Coon Huntin' Story
Bully Has Done Flung a Cravin' on Me
Baby Goes to College
Homecomin' Steaks!
The Graduate Returns
Marcel's Talkin' Chain Saw
The Chauffeur and the Professor
Good Citizenship

MOUTH OF MISSISSIPPI
MCA 47 (selections previously released on Decca album DL7-5342)
Knock Him Out, John
Public School Music Class
The Rat Killin'
Pistol Pete
Those Tigers Are Bad, Wet or Dry
Clower Takes a Trip
Judgment in the Sky
Green Persimmon Wine
Ole Highball
The Meek Shall Inherit the Earth
New-Gene Ledbetter
The Last Piece of Chicken
A Double Fire Place
Little Red

I am a sports fanatic, and I admit to showing my enthusiasm at sporting events. A mother and father can't buy their children's achievements in sports. The kids have to work to excel and earn their own accomplishments. I believe in that. I make a point of attending Southeastern Conference basketball games regularly where I enjoy supporting Mississippi State.

CLOWER POWER
MCAC 317
Second Down and Goal to Go
Ole Brumey Wasn't Runnin' a Coon
The Public School Music Class Learns a Song
I'm That Country
Marcel Says No School Today
Peanut Boilin' Was Required
Life at Route Four—Liberty, Mississippi
How to Back into Show Business
Three Footballs in a Game Ain't Fair
All about Clovis Ledbetter
Marcel Wins a Bet
The Ole Timey Ice Box
Uncle Virsi Ledbetter
Brother Sonny Goes to Church
My Mama Made Biscuits
The Flying Jenny
King Solomon Said
Signaling for a Fair Catch
Little Katy Learns a Lesson
What Christmas Means to Me

COUNTRY HAM
MCA 417
The She Coon of Women's Lib
Panama Limited
The Time We Played Clemson
Marcel Is in Trouble

Mr. Duval Scott
Home in the Country
U.S. Exports
Ole Slantface
The New Fad
My Pet Peeve
Marcel's Invasion
The Young People of Today
All Right
A New Bull
In High Cotton
Be Yourself

LIVE IN PICAYUNE
MCA 486
Live in Picayune
Physical Examination
The Plumber
Bird Huntin' at Uncle Virsi's
Marcel's Snuff
The Tarzan Movie
Rattlesnake Roundup
Aunt Penny Douglas
A Box for Clovis
Marcel Ledbetter Moving Company
The Coon Huntin' Monkey
Marcel's Old Goose
Uncle Virsi's Horse
The Chain
Marcel's Hair Growing Secret
Hot Apple Pie
Soppin' Molasses
New-Gene's 4-H Trip
What's His Number
Counterfeiters
You're Fixin' to Mess Up

THE AMBASSADOR OF GOODWILL
MCAC 782
Titus Plummeritis
Writing in My Bible
Warm Water Heater

170

Tough Nut
Clovis and Beck
The Wise Men
Dig a Dug Well
Marcel Goes Quail Huntin'
It Coulda Been a Lot Worse
Wanna Buy a Possum?
The Headless Man
Flying to the Opry
A Nickel's Worth of Cheese
Marcel's Brother Goes to Jail
Runnin' the Coon
Uncle Virsi Sees the Ocean
Mr. Jake Ledbetter
The Clumsy Mule
The Pet Squirrel
The House I Live In

AIN'T GOD GOOD! (A LAY PREACHING SERMON BY JERRY CLOWER)
Word Records WST-8737
Ain't God Good!
Ain't God Good! (concluded)

ON THE ROAD
MCA 785
Airport Goodbyes
The Hot Hotel
Uncle Virsi's Trial
Rats in the Corn Crib
Clovis Gets a Job
Mr. Duvall Scott's Chicken
Steel Marbles
Tar Baby
Deep Water Baptist
Stealing Teacakes
My First Banana
Hitler on the Front Porch
Fifteen-Yard Penalty
Cutworm Smith
New-Gene and the Lion
My Katy Burns

LIVE FROM THE STAGE OF THE GRAND OLE OPRY
MCA 788
My First Tuxedo
Marcel and the City Fella
The New Chandelier
The Furniture Disease
Clovis Goes to Court
The Resort Hotel
Bunkum Vote
The Burning Building
Claud and the Great War
Funeral Procession
Marcel's Plantation
Boiled Okra
Why Can't Johnny Read
The Johnson Grass
Marcel and the Armadillo
Sittin' up with the Dead

JERRY CLOWER'S GREATEST HITS
MCA 939
A Coon Huntin' Story
Marcel Ledbetter's Moving Company
The New Chandelier
The She Coon of Women's Lib
Newgene and the Lion
The Resort Hotel
Wanna Buy a Possum
Steel Marbles
Marcel's Talking Chain Saw
A New Bull
The Burning Building
Bird Hunting at Uncle Versie's
The Coon Huntin' Monkey
Claud and the Game Warden
The Chauffeur and the Professor
Sittin' up with the Dead

THE LEDBETTER OLYMPICS!
MCA 790
Udell and Ole Skeets
Foot Races, Shot Put, and Concessions

172

The Fox Hunt
The Swimming Event
The Ike and Mike Contest
Do You Love America
Marcel's Dream
Uncle Versie and the Gambler
Where Will You Be When You Get Where You're Going?
Is Anybody Up There?
Uncle Versie's Wreck
Apple Pie and Coffee
Real Love

MORE GOOD 'UNS
MCAC 819
The Maddest Man I Ever Saw
The Dog and the Bear
Holding Pattern
Coon Huntin'
With a Wheelbarrow
The Fish and the Edsel
The Inventory
Computer Pilot
Dove Huntin'
Mr. Doogah
Hi-Ball and the Coon
The Christian Bear
Southern Humor
The Hitchhiker
Clovis' Suit
Two Burnt Ears
The Wealthy Texan
You're on My List

DOGS I HAVE KNOWN
MCA 892
Freckles
Puppy Love
Mike
Little Dogs and Big Dogs
Brummie and the Okra
Nicki
Newgene, the Lying Ledbetter

Old Highball
Ol' Blue
The Magic Wand
The LSU Clock
Employment Office
Loyalty
The Go Gitter
Justice For All

JERRY CLOWER LIVE AT CLEBURNE, TEXAS
MCA 891
Letter From Home
Wooden Leg
Slop!
Coon on De Log
Azlee and Clovis
Udell and the Reverend
Definition of a Cow
Tater Rides the Moped
Turnip Greens
Patch of Peas
Who's the Boss
Zeal
Gathering Votes
The Last Day of School
Attitude

STARKE RAVING!
MCA 952
I Love Small Towns
Green Eyelids
Room 411
Big City Vocabulary
God's Gonna Take Care of Me
Joggers
My Friend Chief Hill
Word Processing
Uncle Versie's Bond
Bill's Vacation
My Grandson Jayree
The Blessing of Giving
How to Order Wine

Crack, W. L. and Rover
Snook's Prey
Owen Cooper Said . . .

AN OFFICER AND A LEDBETTER
MCA 27113
Fox 12 . . . Over . . .
Marines Are Tough
The Marine Recruiter
Our First Banana
Camp Perry
The Civil War
Marcel's Courtmartial
Christmas Dinner
Rat Killings
Catahoula Our Dog
What's That Smell?
Uncle Versie at the Opera
We Was So Poor . . .
Painting the Porch
Baseball Umpire
New Teeth
USO
USS *Bennington*

RUNAWAY TRUCK
MCA 5773
The Trucker and the Lady
Marcel, The Truck Driver
Feudin' Stars
The Pulpit Committee
Peanuts
John Dunn
The Preacher's Water
Two Mean Brothers
The Grassers
How to Tell Time
Runaway Truck
The Baptizing
Negativism
Procto
Sonny and Rambo

Temperance Meeting
A Positive Attitude
Clowerisms
Coon Huntin' on TV
Shake It Off

TOP GUM
MCA 42034
Top Gum
Write It Down
Two-Bit Savings Account
Rules According to Clower
Marcel's Dirty Dozen
Uncle Versie Saves the Day
Fat and Dainty
Broad Bottoms
Horizontal Hitchhiker
Big Mama at the Opry
Grits
Plu-Sha
The Cows in the Corn
School Lunch
Do I Believe?